STAFF FOR THIS BOOK

Editor: Eric Levin

Senior Editor: Richard Burgheim

Art Director: Anthony Wing Kosner

Picture Editor: Christine Ramage

Chief of Reporters: Denise Lynch

Writers: Alfred Gingold, Helen Rogan

Reporter: Aimee Berg

Designer: Scott G. Weiss

Picture Research: Lizette Beltran

Copy Editor: Dennison E. Demac

Art Production: Jason Lancaster

Special thanks to: Alan Anuskiewicz, Michael Aponte, Jane Bealer, Robert Britton, Rachel Cohen, Steven Cook, Orpha Davis, Tom Fitzgibbon, Brien Foy, Susanne Golden, George Hill, Suzy Im, Rachael Littman, Eric Mischel, James Oberman, Stan Olson, Stephen Pabarue, Helen Russell, John Silva, Desirée Yael Vester, Céline Wojtala, the staff of Applied Graphics Technology and the People Edit Tech staff

PRESIDENT: David Gitow
DIRECTOR, CONTINUITIES AND SINGLE SALES: David Arfine
DIRECTOR, CONTINUITIES AND RETENTION: Michael Barrett
DIRECTOR, NEW PRODUCTS: Alicia Longobardo
GROUP PRODUCT MANAGER: Jennifer McLyman
PRODUCT MANAGERS: Christopher Berzolla, Roberta Harris, Stacy Hirschberg, Kenneth Maehium, Daniel Melore
Manager, Retail and New Markets: Thomas Mifsud
ASSOCIATE PRODUCT MANAGERS: Carlos Jimenez, Daria Raehse, Dennis Sheehan, Betty Su, Niki Viswanathan, Lauren Zaslansky, Cheryl Zukowski
ASSISTANT PRODUCT MANAGERS: Victoria Alfonso, Jennifer Dowell, Meredith Shelley
EDITORIAL OPERATIONS DIRECTOR: John Calvano
BOOK PRODUCTION MANAGER: Jessica McGrath
ASSISTANT BOOK PRODUCTION MANAGER: Jonathan Polsky
BOOK PRODUCTION COORDINATOR: Kristen Travers
FULFILLMENT DIRECTOR: Michelle Gudema
ASSISTANT FULFILLMENT MANAGER: Richard Perez
FINANCIAL DIRECTOR: Tricia Griffin
FINANCIAL MANAGER: Amy Maselli
ASSISTANT FINANCIAL MANAGER: Steven Sandonato
MARKETING ASSISTANT: Ann Gillespie

Library of Congress Catalog Card Number: 99-71061

We welcome your comments and suggestions about PEOPLE WEEKLY Books.
Please write to us at:

PEOPLE WEEKLY Books
Attention: Book Editors
PO Box 11016
Des Moines, IA 50336-1016

If you would like to order any of our Hard Cover Collector Edition books, please call us at 1-800-327-6388 (Monday through Friday, 7 a.m.-8 p.m. Eastern Time, or Saturday, 7 a.m.-6 p.m. Central Time).

PREVIOUS PAGE: Harrison Ford as Indiana Jones in *Raiders of the Lost Ark*, 1981

22 We met **ROBIN WILLIAMS** as Mork in '78 and watched his genius morph.

122 **KAREN CARPENTER** and brother Richard smiled away a sad secret in '76.

112
In 1994 the world could still count on **PRINCESS DIANA** to make a joyous splash.

CONTENTS

As They Grow Older, the Greats Keep Getting Better

SEE HOW THEY'VE GROWN

1982 Pumping up at home for *Staying Alive,* Sly Stallone's sequel to *Saturday Night Fever,* the dance-floor peacock spread his wings.

COMEBACK KID
Whether Sweathog, haunted hit man or sweetheart, he lights the screen and makes America care

John Travolta

1991 A passionate flier since age 16, Travolta now pilots, among three other craft in his fleet, this Learjet and his favorite passenger of all—wife Kelly Preston.

"I think I've pretty much gotten what I wanted. Now it's a matter of upkeep."

"I wouldn't know what it's like not to be an icon," says John Travolta. As Vinnie Barbarino, Tony Manero and Danny Zuko, he created three dominating teen images of the 1970s. But one night in 1985, he co-starred in the still photo that perhaps best sums up the coalescence of entertainment and politics that defined the pop culture of the past quarter century. As he danced in the White House with Princess Diana, before the admiring eyes of President Reagan and First Lady Nancy, both former actors, the Age of Celebrity got its close-up. And yet today, at 45, Travolta is bigger than ever—in waistline and box office—all the while remaining the sweet kid from Englewood, New Jersey, with the killer smile and the unique brand of cool.

He began inauspiciously, dropping out at 16 (with the approval of his folks, a drama coach and a tire dealer) to work in commercials and on Broadway. Five years later in *Welcome Back, Kotter,* his Vinnie supplanted the Fonz as America's favorite goofball. By 1977, glittering out of *Saturday Night Fever* posters and album covers, he became the white-suited symbol of the oxymoronic disco culture.

Rough times came too. That same year he lost his great love, Diana Hyland, the 18-years-older actress who'd played his mother in *The Boy in the Plastic Bubble.* His career went south as he kept opting for turkey roles while turning down plums like *An Officer and a Gentleman.* Not until 1989's *Look Who's Talking* did he have a winner. And not until *Pulp Fiction* in 1994 was he back to stay, with a second Oscar nomination (*Saturday Night Fever* was his first) for his portrayal of a melancholy hit man with a bad haircut. "It never occurred to me that my career wasn't salvagable," said Travolta, a rock-steady guy ever wary of drink and drugs.

Travolta credits Scientology for his personal growth. But his anchor is family. He married actress Kelly Preston in 1991; their son was born the next year. "Jett literally has his father spellbound," says Preston, who, with her family, shuttles between homes in California, Maine and Hawaii. "He loves being a movie star," noted Jamie Lee Curtis. He chats easily on the set and with fans, always with that gleam in the eye that makes his characters, good and bad, so appealing. "As a kid, I was a seductive brat," he has admitted. "I loved affection, loved to be held, hugged and kissed. I'm still pretty much the same way."

Oprah Winfrey

COMMUNICATOR IN CHIEF She holds the hearts of all America in her hands

*A*s a celebrity you can make the decision to cut yourself away from the world or be part of it," she says. "I choose to be a part of it. Big time." At 45, the unstoppable phenomenon who is Oprah Winfrey keeps gathering momentum. In the last year alone she has produced and starred in the movie *Beloved,* trounced Texas beef ranchers who had sued her for libel, signed to launch the Oxygen Channel (a new women's cable network), agreed to a $150-million renewal contract for her syndicated show and introduced a self-help concept called "Change Your Life TV." All the while she has continued as host of her daily show and, in her spare time, has worked to help minority children find their place in the world. The wealthiest female entertainer in America ($675 million and counting) and surely the most powerful—one mention in front of her show's 33 million viewers can turn a book into a bestseller—she never for a moment turns her back on the person she once was, the abused and lonely little girl from a broken home in rural Kosciusko, Mississippi.

That connection is the secret of her success. "Your past is a filter that colors your life," she has said. "I believe you need to address it and release it and move on." Indeed she has been tearily out-front with her grim experiences—rape, drug abuse, abortion—even as she has coaxed other people to confront their own. Her candor, abiding weight problems and seeming inability to tie the knot with fiancé Stedman Graham keep her fans rooting for her. However mighty she becomes, Oprah is still a regular person who doesn't have all the answers but won't stop looking. "She really does want to make a difference," says best friend Gayle King, an anchorwoman in Hartford, "and the beauty of it is, she's one of the few people in this country who can."

> **❝ I have a voice to speak to millions of people every day. So how dare I think I can stop? I can't. ❞**

1993 She has collected more than 25 Emmys and has homes in which to display them in Chicago; Florida; Telluride, Colorado; and on her favorite unwinding spot —a 160-acre farm in Indiana.

1984 Three months after Winfrey arrived, *A.M. Chicago*'s ratings overtook *Donahue*.

1985 She won an Oscar nomination for *The Color Purple*, adapted from her favorite book.

1988 Slimmer by 67 pounds, Oprah proudly wheels symbolic fat onstage in a red wagon.

1989 Never married, she has been engaged to businessman Stedman Graham since 1992.

1998 She costarred with Danny Glover in *Beloved*, a rare commercial disappointment.

Tom Hanks

SCREEN GEM Our best-loved actor is frequently surprising, always elusive

The art of Tom Hanks is not letting you see his art. Whether he's playing an oversize adolescent, an AIDS victim or an astronaut, he is so absolutely convincing that it doesn't look like acting. Hanks seems so relaxed, so utterly himself, no matter whom he's playing, that we think we know him. But we don't. Hanks disappears when he acts.

His career path seemed unexceptional at first: theater training, a sitcom, a few movies before his big *Splash* in 1984. It was a good start for a lifetime of light romantic comedies, with no hint of the range and power he would soon demonstrate in *Philadelphia* or *Forrest Gump,* his back-to-back Oscar winners.

How does he delve so deeply into such varied characters? If he knows, he's not telling. Like many natural comedians, he's self-contained. His parents divorced when he was 5, and he moved around a lot with his father, mostly in California. But Hanks dismisses the notion that his peripatetic childhood produced any damage. "Mine was not a broken-down, busted-up family," he says. "Nobody abused anybody."

Now, at 43, he has things the way he wants—writing and directing (*that thing you do!*), producing (the Emmy-winning HBO series *From the Earth to the Moon*) and his pick of parts. Offscreen he leads a quiet, domestic life with Rita Wilson, his second wife of 11 years, and their sons Chester, 8, and Truman, 3. When strangers come up and ask if he's really as nice as he seems, he protests politely, "Hey, now, I'm not always that darned *nice.*" Colleagues beg to differ. Sums up Nora Ephron, the shrewd director of his *Sleepless in Seattle* and *You've Got Mail:* "You wish you knew him, which is a certain kind of movie-star thing that he has."

> **"I think that I have a pretty good handle on myself as an entity in regard to commerce. My strength is, I'm funny."**

1989 In his choice of roles (as well as in this publicity shoot in the canyons of New York City), Hanks is a risk-taker.

1980-82 Cult TV show *Bosom Buddies* put Hanks in drag opposite Donna Dixon.

1988 In *Big,* he found himself a boy trapped in an adult's body—and an Oscar nominee.

1988 His love interest in *Volunteers,* actress Rita Wilson, was his bride three years later.

1993 In *Philadelphia,* he played an ambitious attorney battling homophobia and AIDS.

1994 Hanks's performance as idiot savant *Forrest Gump* moved audiences to tears.

1991 Small and delicate, with piercing blue eyes, Foster has used her vulnerability to create convincing heroines who still play in the movieola of our minds.

Jodie Foster

FILM FORCE A prodigious actress built a unique career and life, directing it her way

> **"** I can't say that being a celebrity is a great thing; there is nothing good about it besides the work. **"**

Jodie Foster was in the audience at the Santa Barbara, California, International Film Festival when host James Wood congratulated her on her pregnancy and crudely joked that the baby's father was "one of the L.A. Lakers." The famously private Foster laughed along with everyone else. And then she cried. It was an uncommon response for a woman who has risen to the top of the business she has been in almost her entire 36 years. Explained Jonathan Kaplan, who directed Foster in *The Accused:* "When you're charged with having to do the work of an adult and you're a child, and it's your responsibility to put bread on the table, crying is out of the question. No one says that to you, but you just know."

Foster learned early, having made her debut bare-tushed in a Coppertone commercial at 3 to help support the family abandoned by her father. By 13, she had done more than 50 TV shows and movies, including *Taxi Driver,* which won her an Oscar nomination (and led an obsessed admirer, John Hinckley Jr., to make an assassination attempt on President Reagan). With a brain to match her acting gifts, Foster soldiered on, graduating magna cum laude from Yale (in lit, not acting) and meticulously picking—and excelling in—the parts she wanted. She also formed a production company and moved into directing with *Little Man Tate* and *Home for the Holidays.* Both movies, she said, "circle around the idea of family and what we do to each other and why we do the things we do to each other."

In 1998 she personally stopped circling and announced she was pregnant (but would not disclose by whom). With the arrival of son Charles, she allowed herself to play the role of first-time mom to the hilt. Foster's friends were thrilled. "It is the most natural thing in the world that she be a mother," said her best buddy, film producer Randy Stone. "She's a kind and generous human being. She's a great listener. This kid is lucky."

1976 Playing a hooker in Martin Scorsese's *Taxi Driver* made her notorious in her teens.

1988 She called her Oscar-winning role as a rape victim in *The Accused* a "turning point."

1991 She had conceptual battles with her producer on *Little Man Tate* and prevailed.

1991 Foster and Anthony Hopkins landed Oscars for the grisly *Silence of the Lambs.*

1998 The proud Beverly Hills mom named her son after Orson Welles's hero in *Citizen Kane.*

Bill Cosby

BIG DADDY A trailblazer,
he broke television boundaries—
but gently and through humor

> **"** I got tired of seeing TV shows that consist of a car crash, a gunman and a hooker talking to a black pimp. **"**

"Stand-up comedian-actor-author-pitchman-multimillionaire philanthropistdoctor of education-executive producer" is how the multi-hyphenate Bill Cosby was once described, but listing his accomplishments doesn't really do him justice. The thing about Cos is that no matter what he does, from hawking Jell-O to writing books, America trusts him.

He has earned our faith by sticking to a few simple rules throughout a career that began in 1962. He is never vulgar. He is never cruel. And he is color-blind. *I Spy,* in which he was the first black man ever to headline a weekly series, made no racial references. Cosby's humor, based on everyday experience and his exuberant imagination, is never topical—it's timeless. It is, unabashedly, family fare. "I'm trying to reach all the people," he once told a reporter. "I want to play John Q. Public."

He has also written three bestselling books and composed music. Raised in a Philadelphia housing project by a mother who worked as a domestic, he dropped out of college but 15 years later got his doctorate in education. His bountiful philanthropies include a $20 million gift to Spelman College.

Cosby is famous as a family man (handling with relative dignity a young woman's claim to be his daughter by one brief fling). Married 35 years to Camille, he is an actively involved father to their four surviving children. The murder of his school-teacher son Ennis in 1997 prompted a tremendous outpouring of sympathy. He is, after all, more than just a beloved entertainer. Cos is, as PEOPLE once wrote, "the dad we all wish we had."

1990 "One of the great faces of the Western world" is how a critic described Cosby; and when that face smiles, which is often, it's just about impossible not to smile too.

1968 The young stand-up collected six consecutive Grammys for his comedy LPs.

1965-68 He also won three back-to-back Emmys costarring with Robert Culp in *I Spy.*

1985 His *Cosby Show* (with Malcolm-Jamal Warner) was No. 1 in the Nielsens for five seasons.

1997 The whole country shared the Cosbys' grief at the murder of their only son, Ennis.

1996- *Cosby* reunited the star with Phylicia Rashad. Madeline Kahn is also onboard.

Madonna

KARMA CHAMELEON She worried mothers until she became one herself

1998 It has been a long, 16-year trip—from Boy Toy, Material Girl, S&M queen, torchy chanteuse and movie star (almost) to serene mom, earnest thinker and pop star reborn.

Can it be true? Is La Ciccone really mellowing, or is this just another tweaking of her myth to fit the Zeitgeist? "Ever since my daughter was born, I feel the fleetingness of time," she lately observed. "And I don't want to waste it on getting the perfect lip color." Or, as her unflappable publicist Liz Rosenberg put it last year, "She's a little bit older. She's evolved, grown-up, matured—and she's not so mad."

This may not be just spin. Take a look at the latest incarnation of Madonna, 40: Gone is that thrusting, beefed-up, Gaultier/Versace-clad, high-gloss persona, and in its place there's a softer-seeming woman with long hair down. She wears less makeup and more clothes. She has moved from her formidable hillside mansion above Los Angeles to an unpretentious house in town. And she has changed her tune about life. "I totally feel like I'm starting over," she has said. The major impetus was the birth of Lourdes in 1996. Finally the raging, rebellious Catholic girl from Bay City, Michigan, was able to move out from under the shadow of her own mother's early death, from breast cancer, when Madonna was only 5. "I knew that having a child would be an incredible healing experience," she has explained, "because I didn't have a mother. I just knew my karma was to have a girl, and I instinctively had a longing for her."

The whole Madonna aura has become kinder and gentler. The once extreme exerciser now practices yoga instead of going to the gym. (Being Madonna, though, she has chosen Ashtanga, the most strenuous form.) The former workaholic studies the Kabbalah (a form of Jewish mysticism that teaches inner peace) and dismisses much of her raunchy, overheated thrashing around in the 1980s as "selfish and disturbingly petulant." Her music also has deepened. The party girl with the Mickey Mouse squeak took voice lessons for her starring role in *Evita,* and in *Ray of Light,* her first huge hit album in years, she expresses her new maturity—both in technique and in her message. Once a bigmouth, the new mother has stopped preaching to the world. As she said, "I just feel like I'm shedding layers."

1982 Slut wannabes idolized this role model. (Their moms were equally unhappy about her 1992 photo book *Sex*.)

1985 The gritty, witty downtown girl of *Desperately Seeking Susan* was a stunning film debut.

1985-89 A SWAT team once had to tame Sean Penn during their fiery marriage.

1993 Exhibitionist and trained dancer, she documented her tour of the Girlie Show.

1998 She says Carlos Leon, the father, will be "ever-present" in Lourdes's life if not her own.

> **" I was a paradox—an outsider and a rebel who wanted to please my father and get straight A's. "**

Steven Spielberg

MASTER OF THE MEDIUM He has become the auteur of our age

Just when we thought we had Steven Spielberg pegged—the Midas behind box office smashes such as *Jaws* and *Jurassic Park,* the special-effects genius who brought comic books to life with the Indiana Jones series, the dreamy sentimentalist of *E.T.* and *Close Encounters of the Third Kind*—he confounded us by showing how much else was going on inside his shaggy head.

It was family that changed him. At 51, he has a total of seven children—one from his first marriage to Amy Irving and the rest with his second wife, Kate Capshaw, whom he wed in 1991. Inexorably the anxious workaholic, who had trouble recovering from his parents' divorce and who said, "I never felt comfortable with myself because I was never part of the majority," has grown up with the rest of the baby boomers and come to terms with his place in the world. Though Spielberg didn't exactly put away childish things—in fact, he revels in the success of producing TV's *Animaniacs*—he has increasingly grappled with themes like society's legacy of racism in such works as *The Color Purple, Amistad* and the mighty *Schindler's List.*

There's no end to his grand plans. Today the nerdy film fanatic, who shot his first feature-length movie at 16, is the billionaire mogul behind DreamWorks SKG, a studio he boldly co-launched in 1994. After a few hits (*Deep Impact, ANTZ*) and some box office disappointments (*Small Soldiers*), DreamWorks has come into its own with *Saving Private Ryan,* Spielberg's heartfelt homage to the generation of his dad, an electrical engineer and WW II bomber crewman. Bounding from one project to another, Spielberg seems fulfilled but still radiates boyish enthusiasm—and apprehension. "Whenever I have a movie coming out," he says, "I am the same nervous blob of misshapen Jell-O that I was when I first began showing those little 8-millimeter films to teeny audiences."

> **"You've no idea how much heat I get from people who want me to go on making *E.T.* over and over again."**

1975 *Jaws* was America's first summer blockbuster, earning $60 million in a month, and the first to get into nine figures.

1982 *E.T. The Extra-Terrestrial* outstripped *Jaws* as the then all-time top grosser.

1993 Spielberg clenched his belated first Oscars (for *Shindler*) with mom Leah Adler and wife Kate Capshaw.

1996 David Geffen, Jeffrey Katzenberg and he redefined moguldom with DreamWorks SKG.

1997 At Universal, he turned a sequel, *The Lost World: Jurassic Park,* into a box office bigfoot that has helped to subsidize larger-hearted, more thematically audacious projects.

1997 He huddled with the grunts on location for *Ryan,* which in '99 won five Oscars.

LEFT: GREGORY HEISLER/OUTLINE. INSETS, FROM TOP: SCREEN SCENES; AARON RAPPORT/OUTLINE; PIETER LESSING/VISAGES; GEORGE LANGE/OUTLINE; PHOTOFEST

Goldie Hawn

CUTIE PIE—She had the smarts to dump the ditz and become a force

Goldie is funny, sexy, beautiful, talented, intelligent, warm and constantly sunny," says playwright Neil Simon. "Other than that she doesn't impress me." Everyone loves Hawn. It has been 29 years since she left television's *Laugh-In,* but the flaxen-haired sweetheart with saucer eyes and helium giggle is still with us. The airhead cast for looking good in a bikini and cracking up when she fluffed a line has become an accomplished actress and producer and a proud mother.

George Schlatter, producer of *Laugh-In,* underestimated Hawn even while singing her praises, declaring, "If you looked inside her head, you would find a pretty little bouquet." Actually you'd find considerable intelligence, which the former college dropout, go-go dancer and Broadway gypsy used to build a career out of a flash in the pan. Hawn, 53, effervesces as naturally on the big screen as she did on the tube. No dummy about money either, she negotiated a percentage of the gross of 1975's *Shampoo.* And when she grew disgusted with the quality of roles coming her way, she became a producer. Her maiden effort, *Private Benjamin,* established Hawn as the bankable star she still is.

Domestic bliss was more elusive than celebrity. A couple of nasty divorces soured her on marriage; but since 1984, when they connected on the set of *Swing Shift,* Hawn has lived with Kurt Russell—unmarried, but very much family. The two are hands-on parents to son Wyatt plus Kate and Oliver Hudson, Goldie's kids by comic Bill Hudson. A practicing Buddhist, Hawn meditates daily. She seems, in short, balanced, and her ability to enchant is as powerful as ever. Son Oliver describes his mother as "a lot like she is in her movies—like champagne, bubbly and floating."

> **There's really nothing not to like about Goldie. For me, she represents the best of life. All I can hope for is to continue being desirable to her.**
>
> KURT RUSSELL

1989 She's a natural on a film set or here in a photographer's studio. But at heart, Hawn has said, "a husband, children and a nice house—that's all I ever wanted out of life."

1968 Her *Laugh-In* character, she said, "is not so much stupid as childlike. She's naive, gullible. I'm like her in many small ways."

1969 It was only her second film, but *Cactus Flower* won her a Best Supporting Oscar.

1980 She also was nominated for *Private Benjamin,* her "comedy with a serious underbelly."

1996 Hawn rampaged with Diana Keaton and Bette Midler— as they played vengeful spurned spouses in *The First Wives Club*.

1997 The clan includes daughter Kate, 20; sons Oliver, 22, and Wyatt, 13; and Russell.

Williams Robin

MANIC IRREPRESSIVE He's the greatest one-man show on earth

1987 At The Improv in New York City, America's least predictable funny man parachutes in and hangs out where he feels most free—onstage—and without a script.

obin Williams, in his initial guise of Mork from Ork, landed on television in 1978. His face was made of rubber, his voice rumbled like a roomful of oddballs. And he wrote his own material, or, rather, it poured out of him—an uninhibited torrent of improvised puns, rude noises and weird imaginings. Virtually overnight, Williams, who'd grown up comfortable but lonely in Bloomfield Hills, Michigan, and San Francisco, the son of an automobile executive and his homemaker wife, was the hottest comic in the land, America's own holy fool.

Today, Williams's revved-up rantings are familiar to children far too young to remember *Mork and Mindy*. They know him as Mrs. Doubtfire or the voice of the antic genie in *Aladdin*. Adults remember him as the ardent English teacher from *Dead Poets' Society*, the healer in *Awakenings* or any of the many roles in which he has hidden his lunatic fires under a tweed jacket or a lab coat. His breakthrough film, *Good Morning, Vietnam*, was little more than an excuse for his hyperkinetic riffing; he could have built a career doing little else. But the Juilliard-trained Williams was too artistically ambitious and audacious to settle; and the Academy noticed, in 1998, honoring him as the shrink in *Good Will Hunting*.

Perhaps Willliams broadened his range because his comedy was just too intense, too exhausting. In younger days he wound down with the traditional Hollywood relaxants, alcohol and drugs. "Cocaine is God's way of telling you you're making too much money," he once remarked ruefully. But the 1982 death of his friend John Belushi shocked him, and he gave up drugs and drinking. The decision coincided with the pregnancy of his first wife, Valerie Velardi. "I knew I couldn't be a father and live that sort of life," he said later.

He's a father now, with two more children by his second wife, Marsha Garces (who once worked as nanny to his first child). At 47, he has grown up in other ways as well. He's the prime mover behind HBO's *Comic Relief,* raising money for the homeless, and he has been a steadfast companion to his old Juilliard buddy Christopher Reeve.

His movie career flourishes, of course. But every so often, late at night, Williams storms the stage of an L.A. club, unannounced, and blows off steam. "It's total freedom, it's mine, my world," he exults. "I can slay the dragon there."

> **" You're only given a little spark of madness. You must not lose that madness. "**

1978-82 Mindy (Pam Dawber) makes nice with Mork, her extra-terrestrial visitor.

1987 Cast as a shock jock and using his own patter, he jolted *Good Morning, Vietnam* to life.

1993 Creating the frumpy Mrs. Doubtfire added four-and-a-half hours to his shooting day.

1998 His proud mom, Laurie, and his wife, Marsha Garces, accompanied him to the Oscars.

1998 For the patients of the antic Patch Adams, laughter was definitely the best prescription.

Brooke Shields

AMERICAN BEAUTY Though pushed into too much too soon, she is today her own boss

> **" I think you can be strong without being bitchy. You can be committed to being intelligent rather than being spoiled. "**

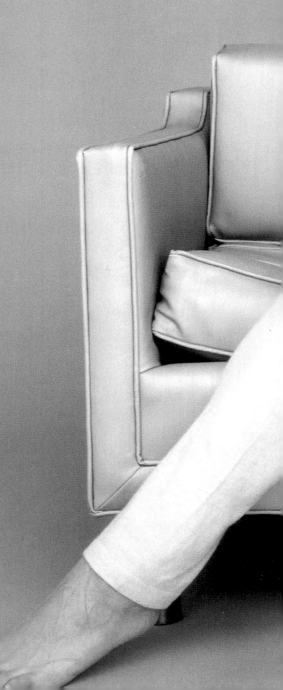

It was just another shoot for an Ivory soap ad, but it made history of a sort. Photographer Francesco Scavullo was given his pick of six different babies— all bawling. Someone in the studio referred him to Teri Shields, who rushed over with her 11-month-old.

"Brooke was smiling in Teri's arms," recalled Scavullo. "She was incredible. I sent all the babies home and just photographed Brooke." Teri, only briefly married to the child's Revlon executive father, was volatile, obsessive and suffered from alcohol problems. But her ambition for her daughter with the picture-perfect look launched a steadily lucrative modeling and movie career. Some of Mom's choices were questionable (the torrid *Endless Love*), some bordered on the pornographic (the Calvin Klein ads), but the game and preternaturally dutiful Shields endured it all with a gorgeous smile. She managed to get herself into Princeton (and out with honors), shunned drugs and announced that she would stay a virgin until she was 20. She was more at home on Bob Hope's TV specials than at Studio 54, where she was sometimes paraded.

With that kind of résumé, you would half expect her to be institutionalized by now. But Shields defied the odds, mastering a buoyant bonhomie. She did finally develop a clear idea of what's right for her and is resolute in achieving it, even to the point, four years ago, of firing her business manager, who happened to be her mother. By that time the coed who had barely dated had found—and, in 1997, married—her unlikely love, shaggy tennis star Andre Agassi. They delighted and encouraged each other, but ultimately his career stagnated while hers sailed. In 1995 she bravely cavorted as Rizzo in a Broadway revival of *Grease* although fresh from bunion surgery. Then, at 34, the Ivy Leaguer found her niche in the silliest of sitcoms. Neither she nor Agassi was willing to sacrifice one's professional goals for the other's emotional needs, and in 1999 they filed for divorce. Shields had wanted children, but as her marriage unwound, she faced facts. "Although there is no perfect time to have children," she said late last year, "I know now is not the time." That is one mark of a grown-up.

1997 Her new solidity has obliterated her past. "I feel fortified," she says, "by the fact that I've weathered it all."

1978 Shields posed naked at 13 in *Pretty Baby*, unleashing a major furor.

1981 Between her and her Calvins there was nothing but a $500,000-plus payday.

1987 A triumph of two tigers: Mom helps celebrate Shields's Princeton graduation.

1997 Shields and Agassi, who split in April 1999, wed in church when he was 27, she, 31.

1998 Judd Nelson plays editor to Shields's scrappy reporter in the sitcom *Suddenly Susan*.

Michael Jordan

HIS AIRNESS The master of our sports universe went up, up and away

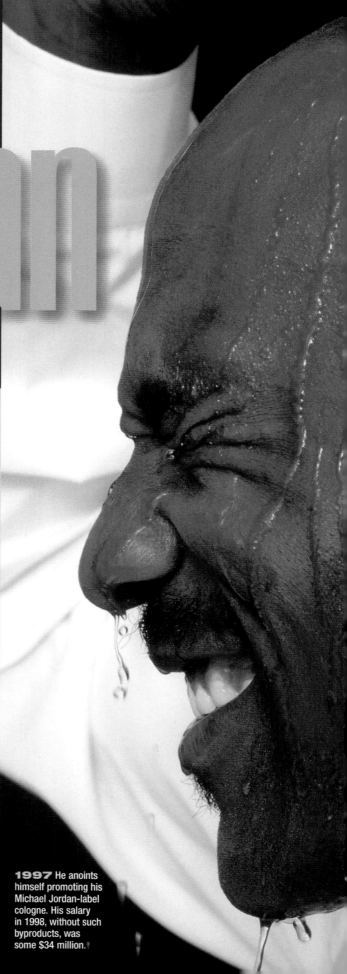

You know what's coming, you know what he's going to do, but you can't stop him," marveled Joe Dumars of the Detroit Pistons. An earlier basketball legend, Larry Bird, called him "God disguised as Michael Jordan." On earth—or in exuberant, indomitable free flight above it—there is no more recognizable nor beloved person extant (with the possible exception of Muhammad Ali). As for the commercial manifestations, FORTUNE estimated (in June 1998) that Jordan had added a very cool $10 billion to the world economy. He himself is said to be worth about $500 million.

In 1999 the self-described "country boy from Wilmington, North Carolina" retired on top at 35. He'd led the NBA in scoring 10 times, and his career per-game average of 31.5 points was the sport's highest. He was named Most Valuable Player after each of the six championships he brought to the Chicago Bulls. He collected half of those title rings after an earlier, brief retirement from basketball and a flier at baseball. As a batter and outfielder, he was not Jordanesque, hitting .202 in the minors.

The man behind those numbers is admirably private. He was very close to his father (who was murdered in 1993), and he keeps his wife of 10 years, Juanita, and their three children out of the limelight. They live outside Chicago in a sprawling, 25,000-square-foot mansion, which includes a full-size basketball court on its grounds. When Jordan can, he heads back to Carolina to hang out and play pick-up hoops with old friends. "It's sad that I'm leaving the game," he concedes, "but it's happy that my life is starting to go into a whole new stage." The world of basketball hopes Jordan will return one more time to the old stage. But out of the spotlight, the holy Bull is pawing the fairways, snorting at the flapping flagstick as at a matador's cape.

1997 He anoints himself promoting his Michael Jordan-label cologne. His salary in 1998, without such byproducts, was some $34 million.

Harrison Ford

MAIN MAN In his crapshoot business, this honest craftsman is Mr. Bankable

1977 Ford was 35 years old and still a struggling actor when *Star Wars* turned him into an overnight sensation.

1984 In *Indiana Jones and the Temple of Doom,* Ford paraded his trademark brown fedora. He still has it.

arrison Ford isn't impressed by the fact that he is the world's biggest box office actor—not only of his time but of all time. "It's what I do for a living," he has said. "It's not my life." Ford had been shuttling in and out of show business for 13 years before *Star Wars* hit. He initially turned down his role in *American Graffiti* because the producers were offering less than he made as a carpenter. Seven blockbusters and numerous lesser hits later, he is modest about his talents. "We're of the show-up-on-time-do-it-and-go-home school of acting," he said at a dinner honoring Sean Connery.

Ford has received only one Oscar nomination in his career (for 1985's *Witness*), but audiences obviously buy the way his decent, jittery, no-frills heroes vanquish preposterous opposition to track down missing treasure or save the free world. His characters possess a detached intensity that emanates from the actor himself. If he seems like a guy who knows what he wants, well, it took awhile. His comfortably middle-class upbringing in suburban Chicago and less than illustrious college career didn't prepare him for the rigors of Hollywood. A first marriage, to his college sweetheart, was a casualty of those years. The second time around, Ford has been an involved parent to his second pair of children (with his wife of 16 years, screenwriter Melissa Mathison, who wrote *E.T. The Extra-Terrestrial* and *Kundun*). He juggles his career around his family, rarely making more than one film a year. Avoiding Hollywood, they live in New York City and on their 800-acre ranch in Wyoming.

He is genuinely surprised that, at 57, he's still a heart-throb. A single earring is a small nod to fashion, but on the whole, Ford is publicly inconspicuous, as befits a man who declared that the most important things in life are: "Kids. A good bed. Good shoes. Practical clothing. And time for yourself."

> " Harrison Ford is the way that we would be if we could be our most heroic selves. "
>
> DIRECTOR PHILLIP NOYCE

1985 Ford and wife Melissa Mathison, both Buddhists, had an audience with the Dalai Lama.

1997 As the President in *Air Force One,* he saved the world from the likes of Gary Oldman.

1998 He and Anne Heche ignored the fuss over her gayness, his geezerdom in *Six Days*.

LEFT: NIGEL PERRY/CPI. INSETS, FROM TOP: IPOL INC.; REX USA; ARCHIVE PHOTOS/POOL/REUTERS; SCREEN SCENES; TIMOTHY WHITE/KOBAL COLLECTION

> "I love comedy, but serious is closer to who I am—I know pain, I really know it."

1998 For the record, Cher maintains that her only plastic surgery has been to get her nose and teeth fixed plus having her breasts firmed up—three times.

Cher

MERCURIAL GIRL Romantic, nervy yet vulnerable, she's a neo-Bohemian

1966 Cher's loud contralto and Sonny's undistinguished tenor clicked on the charts.

1983 Multitalented Cher broke through in a new medium when Mike Nichols cast her with Meryl Streep in *Silkwood*.

1987 Acting up a storm as a frumpy Brooklyn bookkeeper in *Moonstruck*, she won moody baker Nicolas Cage's heart.

1991 After *Mask*, Cher became involved with sufferers of neurofibromatosis.

1998 With gay activist daughter Chas, she gave an emotional eulogy at Sonny's funeral.

"It's silly to pretend that you can be talented and rich and not messed up," Cher once said in her forthright fashion. "Usually the three go together. But even with all the mistakes that I've made, I still respect who I am." So, in a way, do we all. She has served as our national free spirit to divert and cheer us through uptight times. Cherilyn Sarkisian first showed up on our radar at 19 in the thrall of husband Sonny Bono. She was sardonic and skinny, with a face like a Modigliani, courtesy of her Armenian-French-Native American heritage. She decided to be famous the moment her mom took her to see *Dumbo* when she was 4: "I looked at the screen and said, 'That's what I want to do.'"

Five decades after that epiphany, Cher has made her share of missteps, including a nine-day marriage to Gregg Allman and that notorious hair-care infomercial; yet she has enjoyed more fame than she could have imagined. After a couple of hit singles ("Baby Don't Go" and "I Got You, Babe"), she became a campy cult figure with CBS's *The Sonny and Cher Comedy Hour* (1971-74). Ten years later she picked herself up after jettisoning Sonny, cut short an unsatisfying though lucrative ($300,000 a week) Vegas career and essayed acting. She turned out to be a natural. Her wonderfully unassuming performances won her raves and an Oscar for *Moonstruck*. Following the eccentric dictates of her heart, Cher cloaked herself in outrageous Bob Mackie plumage, created a perfume, peddled pseudo-medieval furniture through a catalog and fell for younger men like guitarist Richie Sambora and Rob Camilletti, the 27-year-old bagel baker whom she met on her 40th birthday and lived with for three years. She found them a welcome change from the often-intimidating Bono. "They've been raised," she once observed, "by women who are just like me. Younger men are more supportive and a lot less demanding."

As she approached 53, Cher didn't have a special guy in her life, and she had begun to excise her tattoos; but otherwise she was on a roll with a No. 1 single ("Believe"), movies afoot and a solid relationship with her kids Chastity Bono and Elijah Blue Allman. She remains a piece of work in perpetual progress.

1961 Howard was acting onstage and before the cameras just as soon as he could walk. "I'm someone who grew up in front of other people's eyes," he said.

Ron Howard

BOY WONDER A kid wiz avoids the skids, hits the top and yet hangs on to his values

reatively, the man's a volcano!" exclaimed Henry Winkler in 1978. The Fonz didn't know the half of it. By that time, the freckled, baby-faced actor had been toiling in movies and TV for 23 of his 24 years but hadn't yet broken through as the director of such provocative films as *Splash, Cocoon, Parenthood, Apollo 13* and *EDtv.* Howard performed in his first movie at the age of 18 months and became a star at 5, playing the soulful Opie on *The Andy Griffith Show.* Despite

1973 George Lucas's *American Graffiti* was a star factory, also launching Richard Dreyfuss and Harrison Ford.

1974-80 Howard and Henry Winkler propelled *Happy Days* to the top of the ratings and spun off *Laverne & Shirley*.

1995 Rumpled and balding, Howard still reminds his fans of Opie. "When people recognize me," he observed, "there's a warmth that I really appreciate."

1984 Howard established his directing chops and launched Daryl Hannah as Tom Hanks's mermaid love in *Splash*.

1995 He rehired Tom Hanks (with Kevin Bacon) for his space odyssey *Apollo 13*.

growing up in Burbank with actors for parents, he lived a regular life, attending public schools and playing sports in between learning his lines. His father, Rance, told him, "You prepare, do it and go home. It's a job, same as a paperboy."

That sense of purpose has permeated Howard's professional life. In the 1970s, while starring in the sitcom *Happy Days* and the movie *American Graffiti,* he was also hanging around with directors such as George Lucas, soaking up skills. The movies with which he subsequently made his name are smart, warmhearted and unpretentious, just like the man himself. Now 45, Howard lives with his writer wife (and high school sweetheart), Cheryl Alley, and their four children in a New York City suburb. It's the only kind of life he's comfortable with. "I went through a period where I thought I should rebel," he confesses. That lasted "about a week. It really wasn't me." Incidentally, his kids go to public school, just the way Dad did.

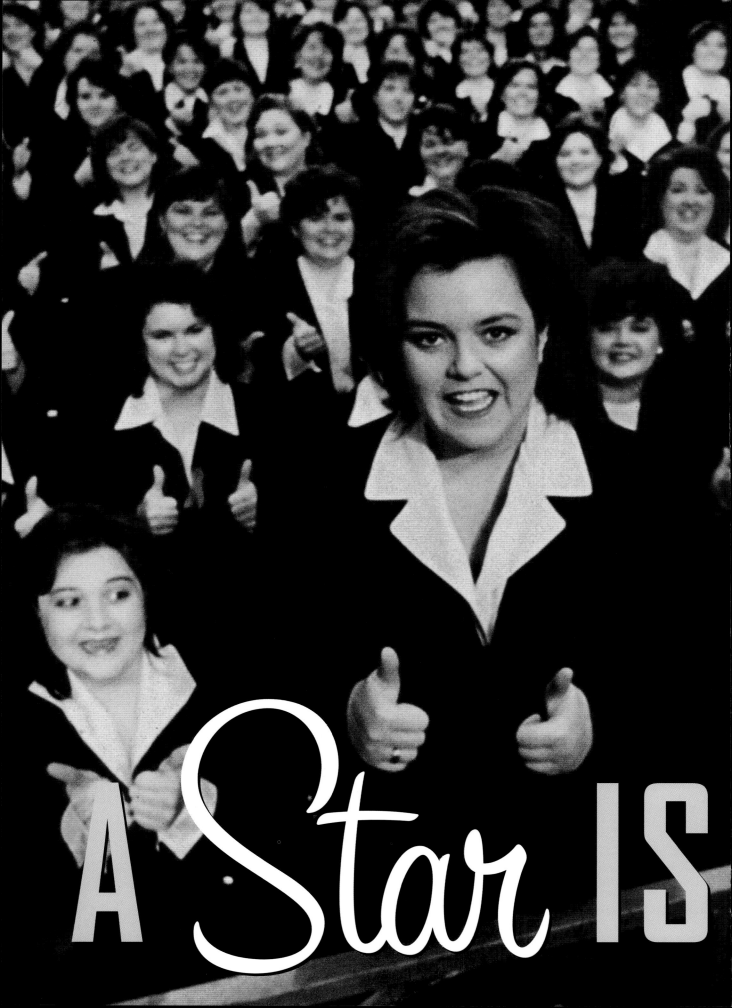

A Star IS

BORN

Breakthrough performances or bold ideas can propel a new fave into the firmament

Rosie O'DONNELL

A stand-up reinvented herself as Queen of Nice

O'Donnell wanted to keep normal hours for her son (now she has a daughter too), so the once-tough club comic moved from movies (*A League of Their Own, Beautiful Girls*) to TV, creating a talk show that would hark back to the gentle style of Dinah Shore, Merv Griffin and Mike Douglas. Growing up in a working-class home on Long Island, New York, she had been glued to the tube, especially after her mom died when O'Donnell was 10. The TV was "a surrogate parent, a friend," she'd figured, and she revived that chumminess on a show that now trails only *Oprah* and *Jerry Springer* in daytime-talk ratings. No sleazy revelations or embarrassing confrontations here. Instead the stars bask in the admiration of O'Donnell, 37, and the audience gets to enjoy Ring-Dings and milk—or, as in her 1996 debut year, to impersonate their beloved host.

Bruce SPRINGSTEEN

This rocker was born to be The Boss

"I always saw a lot of myself in my audience," he once said, and they reciprocated, notably at his go-for-broke concerts (like this 1976 gig) that lasted hours and left fans as spent as his kick-butt E Street Band. Now Bruce Springsteen is 50. Divorced from model Julianne Phillips, he's remarried and has three kids with sympatico, blue-collar bandmate Patti Scialfa. His recent music is quiet, introspective. But for millions, Bruce still embodies the irresistible, unquenchable force of rock and roll.

LEFT: GLOBE PHOTOS; RIGHT, FROM TOP: SNOWDON/CAMERA PRESS/RETNA LTD.; SUZANNE VLAMIS/AP; AP

Mikhail BARYSHNIKOV

Freedom allows a great artist to soar

For him, boundaries are to be crossed. Or leaped. When Mikhail Baryshnikov defected to the West in 1974, the ballet star with the peerless technique gave up a privileged life in Russia to take his chances here. He also has been a risk-taker in movies, TV and the stage, not to mention romance with the likes of ballerina Gelsey Kirkland and Jessica Lange (with whom he has a daughter). At 51, he's old for dance but still performs, maintaining, "It is excruciating pleasure—and pain at the same time."

Nadia COMANECI

Gymnastics found new perfection

A tiny, unsmiling, 14-year-old gymnast from Romania electrified the 1976 Montreal Olympics by winning seven perfect scores, three gold medals, and a silver and a bronze. After difficulties getting re-rooted, Nadia Comaneci wed U.S. gymnast Bart Conner and now coaches at his school in Oklahoma.

SATURDAY NIGHT LIVE:
the Seventies

THE ORIGINAL CAST
The gifted young comics who brightened NBC's *Saturday Night Live* in its best and boldest decade were (clockwise from top left) Laraine Newman, John Belushi, Jane Curtin, Chevy Chase, Dan Aykroyd, Gilda Radner and Garrett Morris.

Revolutionizing staid sketch TV, the show became a fame factory for its Players

It began in TV's Square Age. As producer Lorne Michaels prepared for *SNL*'s 1975 debut, he had to deal with a host—comedian George Carlin—who planned to wear jeans and a T-shirt; and with a network that wanted him in a suit. The compromise: a suit with a T-shirt. And, said Michaels, "Western civilization as we know it did not end." But something did change. Delighted viewers relished the show's radically new, raw, fast-paced mix of merciless parodies of current events (and the medium itself) as well as sketches whose characters became household names. So, too, did its supposedly Not Ready for Prime Time Players, who parlayed *SNL* gigs into crossover careers (see pages 51 and 75). As one of them famously put it, "I'm Chevy Chase, and you're not."

WILD AND CRAZY GUYS The Festrunk Brothers (in '85) were created in 1977 by Aykroyd (left) and frequent host Steve Martin, 54, antic actor and writer.

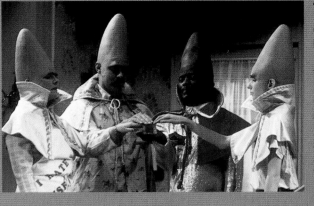

THE CONEHEADS
Curtin, Aykroyd and Newman (with Morris in '78) played aliens from the planet Remulak who insisted, "We are from France." All three appeared in the '93 film *Coneheads*. Aykroyd, 47, starred in *The Blues Brothers* and *Ghostbusters* flicks and cofounded the House of Blues empire.

THE KILLER BEES
In or out of the bee costume he hated at first, Belushi (with Walter Matthau in '78) had sting. As an apoplectic samurai, a mock Joe Cocker or raging on "Weekend Update," he was the Player you had to watch.

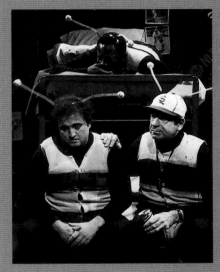

THE LOUNGE SINGER
Seedy and ingratiating (in '82), Bill Murray, 48, would work a room to death. He later was in the *Ghostbusters* movies and won raves for *Groundhog Day* and 1998's *Rushmore*.

CHEESEBURGER
At the Olympia Restaurant, Curtin, Newman and Radner (in '78) needed strong constitutions to cope with tyrannical owner Pete (Belushi) and his limited menu. Curtin, 52, also played the "Weekend Update" anchorwoman but left *SNL* after five seasons. She later headlined (with Susan Saint James) the sitcom *Kate & Allie*.

Pope
JOHN PAUL II

A shepherd tended his worldwide flock

In 1978, Karol Wojtyla became the first non-Italian Pope in 455 years (here in Rome, days after his elevation). His open support of his native Poland's Solidarity movement helped to crack the Iron Curtain. And not even a 1981 assassination attempt could stop him from spreading his uncompromising but sympathetic message. The best-traveled of all Popes, he remained on the road at 79.

Penny MARSHALL

She whined, and millions laughed

The gum-snapping, wise-cracking Laverne of Penny Marshall (right, in 1976) and Cindy Williams's kinder, gentler Shirley were once TV's funniest blue-collar broads. Marshall went on to direct hits such as *Big* and *A League of Their Own.* Now 55, divorced (from Rob Reiner) and a grandma, she's that Hollywood rarity, a bankable female director.

Andy KAUFMAN

A world-class weirdo sadly left us

He lip-synched the *Mighty Mouse* theme, wrestled with women and took an audience out for milk and cookies. Andy Kaufman's oddball persona flourished on TV as Latka Gravas, the Slavic "mirage mechanic" of *Taxi* (here in 1982, two years before his death of cancer, at 35). One of many comics inspired by his wild spirit, Jim Carrey is playing Kaufman in a screen bio.

Sylvester STALLONE

This underdog whupped the odds

The writer-actor's stardom rests on two franchise roles: Rocky (right, with Talia Shire, in 1976) and Rambo (above, in '82), sensitive guys with big chips on beefy shoulders. At 53, he keeps trying new things—comedy, character parts, a third marriage. Audiences preferred Sly hanging tough and taking no prisoners.

Meryl STREEP

She's the leading actress of our day

Her haunting face carried *Kramer vs. Kramer* (1979), winning Streep her first Oscar as a wife who leaves husband Dustin Hoffman and son Justin Henry (left). Chameleonlike, she won a second Oscar as a Polish woman in *Sophie's Choice* and by now, at 50, has been nominated for nine more.

Stephen KING

Who knows what evil lurks? He does

By the time his second novel, *Salem's Lot*, became a miniseries in 1979, he had published three more. Today his output exceeds 40 volumes and more than 30 TV or film properties. Stephen King, 52, has a theory as to why his weird tales of ordinary folks, like his Maine neighbors, affect us so: "We make up horrors to help us cope with the real ones."

Lech WALESA

A working-class hero expelled Marxism

In 1980, Lech Walesa, a 37-year old, out-of-work electrician, joined the Gdansk shipyard strike, helped found the Solidarity labor movement and set in motion the process that would overturn the Communist regime in Poland. Blunt-spoken and ill-educated, he survived prison terms and the disdain of the intelligentsia to become president of a free and reborn Poland 10 years later.

Miss PIGGY

"Look at *moi.* I'm in pig heaven!"

With *The Great Muppet Caper* (1981), the divinely cantankerous and glamorous Miss Piggy achieved the icon status she'd craved. For the previous 10 years she'd been just one of the gang on Jim Henson's *Sesame Street.* Moved to the Muppets' spinoff, she blossomed, and so did her love for that (justifiably) jumpy frog Kermit.

Ted KOPPEL

An anchor gives it to us straight

He had been in news biz 16 years when the 1979 Iran hostage crisis thrust him into the anchor spot on ABC's "temporarily permanent" 11:30 ET analysis show. Two decades later, *Nightline's* still there. So is Ted Koppel, 59, still unflappably focused, still asking the questions we would ask if we could think of them.

PRINCE

By any name, the Artist endures

Already at 12 the Minneapolis kid had mastered more than 20 instruments, and his explicit lyrics and raunchy performances made him a star by the time of this '84 gig. At 41, he lives with one of his dancers, has taken a glyph for a name and is more productive than ever. Yet he's still ready to party like it's 1999.

Richard SIMMONS

Thin's in, thanks to an elfin televangelist

"Fat people die young," the anonymous note said, and 268-lb., 5'7" Richard Simmons, 19, took the hint, dieting himself at first into anorexia. By 1983 (below) he had turned his fitness-as-fun gospel into a TV hit. On video he sold in the millions, helped by the 100-plus annual mall appearances the unstoppable Simmons still makes at 51.

Mel GIBSON

A road warrior takes Tinseltown

In 1981, Mel Gibson, 25, burned up the screen as Mad Max in *The Road Warrior* (left). A ruggedly charming prankster with a happy marriage and seven children, the U.S.-born Aussie could have coasted on the follow-up success of the *Lethal Weapon* series. Instead he chose to direct, and his *Braveheart* won five Oscars, including Best Director and Best Picture.

Mary Lou RETTON

She raised the bar for American women

This ferociously determined 16-year-old from West Virginia grabbed the all-around gold at the 1984 Los Angeles Olympics—the first U.S. woman gymnast ever to win an individual medal—with a stylish combination of power and exuberance. Mary Lou Retton then reaped a tide of endorsements (from Wheaties to Vidal Sassoon) and a joyous second act as motivational speaker, wife of Shannon Kelley (a football star turned business man) and mother of two.

Bill GATES

He opened Windows to change the world

A bored Harvard dropout, Bill Gates developed MS-DOS in 1980, just before PCs hit the market, and he had the savvy to retain ownership of the software. Today, 90 percent of the world's computers run Microsoft programs, and the geek tycoon (here in 1984) became the richest man in America. His hardball practices provoked lawsuits. But Gates, mellower, married and a father at 43, has insisted, "Our success is based on only one thing: good products."

Arnold SCHWARZENEGGER

A muscular Austrian became U.S. royalty

An émigré from Graz, Austria, with the physique of a god, Arnold Schwarzenegger, 52, parlayed bodybuilding fame into screen success in 1977 with *Pumping Iron* (above) and various bone-crusher roles, culminating in *The Terminator* (left, in 1984). Two years later the smart, witty Republican wed Maria Shriver, a Kennedy Democrat.

Dr. Ruth WESTHEIMER

She's a pedagogue of happy hanky-panky

This diminutive (4'7") daughter of Holocaust victims has packed a lot of experience into her 71 years. A thrice-married mother of two, she was a freedom fighter in Israel and a housemaid in New York City, but she made her name, Dr. Ruth Westheimer, as the media's most outspoken, ubiquitous (here in '86) and compassionate sex therapist.

Sarah FERGUSON

The redhead was too raucous to be royal

The 1986 wedding seemed a perfect match between the extroverted Prince Andrew and "Fergie," a vivacious commoner (right, in '86). But in 1992, pictures surfaced of her topless, toe-sucking dalliance with a Texas financial adviser—as her two daughters looked on. The marriage ended in 1996, and the ex-Duchess, now 39, shills for firms such as Weight Watchers.

BILLY CRYSTAL AND MARTIN SHORT
Crystal's Latin smoothie, Fernando, always stroked guests, purring, "You look maaahvelous," with suave conviction, even in this 1985 sketch where the visitor was Short's cowlicked loon, Ed Grimley Jr. Short, 49, went on to Broadway success, and Crystal, 51, became a film star and a masterful Oscar host.

DENNIS MILLER
He raised the bile to new levels on "Weekend Update." Miller (in 1989) treated world eminences, from Khomeini to Reagan, with equal measures of contempt and ridicule. No mellower now at 45, he continues to rant on his own cultish HBO show.

EDDIE MURPHY
The manic cool that Murphy brought to characters like rubbery-but-grouchy Gumby (in 1982) bounced him up to big-screen superstardom in *Beverly Hills Cop* and now, at 38, back to the tube as producer/creator of *The PJs*.

JON LOVITZ
The plummy Master Thespian stole a scene even from Glenn Close (in '89). Much in demand at 42, he's on TV's *NewsRadio* and has been cast by Woody Allen in his next movie.

THE CHURCH LADY
Dana Carvey's insufferably smug creation (in '91) was almost believable, whether primly boogying to the organ or wondering if her *Church Chat* guest were not involved with SATAN. He also morphed into George Bush, Ross Perot and a sadistic, Schwarzenegger-esque, Austrian fitness guru named Hans. Now 44, Carvey has twice undergone heart surgery.

MONSTERS
One of *SNL*'s bizarre traditions, begun in the 1980s, was a running riff in which Lovitz was cast as Tonto, Kevin Nealon as Tarzan and Phil Hartman as Frankenstein (grunting geekily in 1990).

This duo showed us the dark side of passion

Glenn CLOSE

Close, as the one-night stand who wouldn't go away, and Douglas, as the object of her relentless affection, gave a new meaning to "unsafe sex." Their vehicle, *Fatal Attraction*, was a blockbuster in 1987. Michael, now 55, and Glenn, 52, have had numerous successes since, but to many fans they'll always be that hot couple groping each other in the elevator.

Michael DOUGLAS

Patrick SWAYZE

We swooned at his sultry moves

A classically trained Broadway hoofer with a buff body, Patrick Swayze became a world-class heartthrob at 35 with *Dirty Dancing* (1987), which also starred Jennifer Grey (pre-nose bob). This gentle, happily married Texan followed up with the romantic 1990 tearjerker *Ghost*.

Kevin COSTNER

A Gary Cooper wore his heart on his sleeve

At 33, he achieved leading-man status in *Bull Durham* (1988) and followed up with another baseball drama, *Field of Dreams* (below). But the lanky, laconic Costner's creative breakthrough came in *Dances with Wolves,* a Sioux-celebrating western that he also directed. It won seven Oscars, including Best Picture of 1990.

LEFT: PARAMOUNT PICTURES/FOTO FANTASIES; RIGHT, CLOCKWISE FROM TOP: EMILE ARDOLIHO/SYGMA; KOBAL COLLECTION; MELINDA SUE GORDON/UNIVERSAL/MPTV

Macaulay CULKIN

This little-boy-lost found his fortune

He'd already acted with Burt Lancaster in *Rocket Gibraltar*, but it was 1990's *Home Alone* (above) that propelled the impish 10-year-old with the panicky look to stardom. After earning $5 million for *Home Alone 2*, he got in the middle of a family feud before marrying actress Rachel Miner at 17.

Nelson MANDELA

A rebel becomes a world statesman

Freedom "is an ideal I hope to live for and achieve," Nelson Mandela said in 1964, "but it is an ideal for which I am prepared to die." After 27 years in South African prisons, he emerged a free man in 1990 (above), ready at age 72 to lead his country into a future that would redress Apartheid.

Matt GROENING

His satire crossed the line

Matt Groening's first foray into animation in the late '80s, *The Simpsons,* didn't just enter the mainstream. In the '90s it *became* the mainstream, a juggernaut of ratings and merchandising that has made Groening, 45, superrich. Not bad for a cartoonist who began with an underground newspaper strip titled *Life in Hell.*

Norman SCHWARZKOPF

The Bear roared, and Saddam ran for cover

When then 56-year-old Stormin' Norman Schwarzkopf led U.S. forces to victory in Operation Desert Storm in 1991, he liberated the Kuwaitis from Iraqi occupation with minimal Allied casualties. His triumph and endearing persona—a bluff father figure devoted to his troops, his dogs and gourmet cooking—made the general an instant American hero.

BEFORE

PRODUCTION PLANT SEVERELY DAMAGED

Colin POWELL

He was the Gulf War's mastermind

The son of Jamaican immigrants, Gen. Colin Powell became the youngest—and first black—Chairman of the Joint Chiefs of Staff. In 1991, at 53, he planned, oversaw and briefed America on the Iraqi campaign with such reassuring modesty and skill that he later disappointed many (but pleased his wife) by not running for President.

Garth BROOKS

He took country to town

Small wonder he looked smug in 1991. That year, Garth Brooks's third album, *Ropin' the Wind,* entered both country and pop charts at No. 1—not bad for a former bouncer, college jock and advertising major. By now, at 37, he has racked up U.S. sales of 89 million. Only the Beatles have sold more.

Pamela ANDERSON

She was much too sexy for her shirt

As *Home Improvement*'s first Tool Girl she was noticed, but *Baywatch* made her famous. Few filled out a Speedo like Pamela Anderson (here, in '94). Her *Playboy* appearances, tumultuous marriage to rocker Tommy Lee and notorious honeymoon video buffed her bad-girl image. Now 32, the mother of two had her implants removed so (as a 34C) she can wear couture in her new TV show, *V.I.P.*

Sharon STONE

This sassy blonde loves to shock us

"We Barbie dolls are not supposed to behave the way I do," said Sharon Stone, 41. She was discussing her feisty intelligence, not the naughty, pantieless, leg-crossing scene in *Basic Instinct* (1992) that made her notorious. As for her behavior, think old-style movie star—imperious, vampy—but interesting in new ways. Wed to newspaper editor Phil Bronstein in '98, she raises big bucks for AIDS research.

Katie COURIC

Even Bryant Gumbel respected her

Katie Couric, 42, looks like a pixie (left, in '93), but fans of *Today,* which she has cohosted since 1991, relish the gusto of her exchanges with, say, George Bush or an irascible Yasir Arafat. Couric's poise and inner strength were just as solid when her lawyer husband, Jay Monahan, died of cancer in 1998 and she carried on.

Tim ALLEN

Real men get real laughs and ratings

When Tim Allen developed his hairy-chested show in response to the men's movement, it sprouted. Not even revelations of a 28-month jail term that Allen had served on cocaine charges back in the early 1980s could stop *Home Improvement*'s momentum. It rose to No. 1 in the Nielsens in 1993 (right). This season, its eighth, is its last, but Allen, 46, has nothing to worry about. As the show's first director, John Pasquin, has noted, "Men like him, women and kids . . . even armadillos like him."

ER
They found the Rx for success

With its jerky, handheld cameras, rapid-fire jargon and ample gore, *ER* isn't always easy to watch. The cast, however, *is,* even when confronting tough issues such as AIDS, a son's deafness or a waiting room full of accident victims. Not that they can't clown (as at right, in 1994).So popular is *ER*—which never finished a season lower than second in the ratings—that even the departure of resident dreamboat George Clooney barely hurt. It has just meant more face time for callow Carter (Noah Wyle), fiery Benton (Eriq LaSalle) and sensitive Greene (Anthony Edwards), the soul of the show. But it's the ensemble that makes *ER* essential viewing.

Marcus Welby was never like this (from left: Wyle, Edwards and Clooney).

Jerry SEINFELD
Behold the master of his domain!

By 1995 (below), *Seinfeld* had burrowed deep into our national psyche. Six years into its nine-season run, the show had created its unique iconography (like the star's puffy shirt) and a cast of pitiable if irresistible characters. Jerry Seinfeld, 45, a stand-up comic and a legendary perfectionist, grossed $267 million in the farewell year, but enough was enough. "The show's overwhelmed my life completely," he said, shortly before seining off in '98.

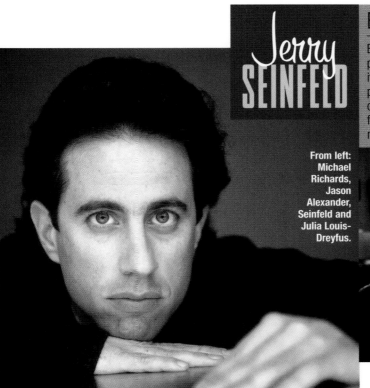

From left: Michael Richards, Jason Alexander, Seinfeld and Julia Louis-Dreyfus.

Brad PITT

A legion of ladies fell for this legend

The Oklahoma native doffed his shirt and stole the show in *Thelma & Louise.* He affirmed his stardom in 1994's *Legends of the Fall* (left) as a cowboy with a tortured soul. Courteous and down-to-earth, Brad Pitt, 35, is bewildered by his hunk status. His ladyloves (in chronological order): Robin Givens, Juliette Lewis, Gwyneth Paltrow and Jennifer Aniston.

Sandra BULLOCK

A sweetheart sped into superstardom

It was a standard girl's part in a standard thriller, but by the end of *Speed* (1994), the world was crazy for Sandra Bullock, bus driver extraordinaire. Now 35, a full-fledged leading lady and comedienne, Bullock retains the wholesome, unaffected charm that got her voted "most likely to brighten your day" in her Arlington, Virginia, high school.

Jim CARREY

He turned yucks into megabucks

America loved Jim Carrey's manic, take-no-prisoners comedy in 1994's *Ace Ventura.* (above). He also scored that year in *The Mask* and *Dumb & Dumber* and became a $20-million-a-movie man. Now 37, he has proved he can act, in *The Truman Show,* but clowning is his art form.

FRIENDS

Clockwise from top left, in 1995: LeBlanc, Aniston, Perry, Cox, Kudrow and Schwimmer.

The X-FILES

Something paranormal this way comes

A cult hit since its 1993 premiere, this spooky series swiftly became an obsession. It featured dense, challenging plots and the understated intelligence of David Duchovny and Gillian Anderson as agents Mulder and Scully (below). Explaining its soul, creator Chris Carter said, "I'm a nonreligious person in search of religious experience."

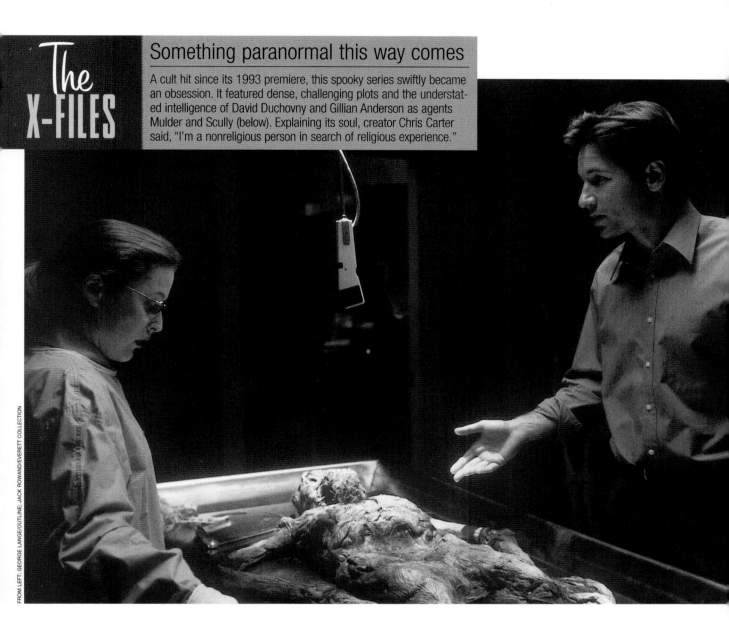

Their ensemble act proved a career springboard for a promising sextet

The six engaging young actors couldn't have wished for a more glittering showcase. Courteney Cox, now 35, with her striking blue eyes and black hair, already had some face recognition (she'd boogied in a Bruce Springsteen video), and all the others had at least guested on prime-time series. But the sitcom-smash *Friends,* which made its debut in 1994, gave them the chance to look great, speak funny lines and play off each other to greater advantage. Small wonder that their opportunities (and salaries) blossomed. Lisa Kudrow, 36, a sweet eccentric with hair-trigger timing, got to exhibit her comic gifts in movies such as *Analyze This.* Appealing Jennifer Aniston, 30, has had her splashiest role in *The Object of My Affection*—and maybe her happiest one subsequently as Brad Pitt's steady. Cox showed up in *Scream* and its *2,* and David Schwimmer, 32, used his hangdog charm to considerable effect in *The Pallbearer.* Matthew Perry, 30, and Matt LeBlanc, 32, are also piling up a bunch of big-screen credits. Clearly they have all gotten a little help from *Friends.*

Martha STEWART

She built a tidy empire on home ec

Growing up in a Polish-American family in Nutley, New Jersey, Martha Stewart, now 58, was required to make her clothes and paint her room; and at 10, she began planning children's parties. By 1996, when she was ruling this Long Island roost (among three other homes), the driven divorcée was as famous for her workaholic, perfectionist ways as for the magazine, books, TV shows and mail-order millions her conglomerate had generated.

Shania TWAIN

This country artist lived the life she hymns

Her name means "on my way" in Ojibwan, and she chose it to honor her Native American stepfather. Shania Twain, 34, started on her way as a teen singing in local Ontario bars, then took time off in her 20s to raise three siblings after her folks' death in a car accident. In 1995, with the help of her producer-husband Robert John "Mutt" Lange, Twain made *The Woman in Me*, the breakthrough album that established her as country's sexiest new star.

Prince WILLIAM

The handsome heir to the throne grows into the part

Gallantly claiming to like even the tailcoated garb, the shy, 13-year-old Prince William of Wales (his tracksuit bears the letters W.O.W.) strode beaming into his first day at elite Eton College on September 7, 1995. Over the next three years he shot up to more than 6', excelled in academics and sports, developed an interest in girls and, as the world knows, coped with the death of his beloved mum, Princess Diana, in 1997, with the dignity of a true prince.

Dolly
THE SHEEP

There *could* be another ewe (or you)

In 1997, English embryologist Ian Wilmut stirred the world, and considerable controversy, by cloning Dolly the sheep from one ewe's cell. "I don't have sleepless nights," he said of the ethical questions. "I believe we are a moral species." Dolly (admiring herself in '98) now plays hostess to tourists and school kids at her home in Scotland.

JEWEL

A frontier babe came in from the cold

It sounds made up, but it's all true: Jewel (Kilcher) is her real name. The angel-faced folkie did grow up in an Alaskan log cabin without running water, did yodel with her performer parents at local hotels from age 6 and then did live out of a van (in San Diego in 1996). The year before, at 21, she released her first album, *Pieces of You,* and by touring nonstop, did turn it into a multi-platinum hit.

Matt DAMON

Ben AFFLECK

Two actors penned their way out of penury

"Ben and I wrote the script out of frustration," Matt Damon, 28, says of *Good Will Hunting,* his film with Massachusetts pal Ben Affleck, 27. That got the struggling actors juicy roles and brief romances with Minnie Driver (Matt) and Gwyneth Paltrow (Ben). "I thought I was remarkably composed," said Affleck of sharing the '97 original screenplay Oscar, "considering I nearly wet my pants."

Tara LIPINSKI

Tinker Bell brings the U.S. the gold

At the 1998 Nagano Olympics, all 4'11" and 82 pounds of Tara Lipinski leaped and pirouetted into first place (to her coaches' glee, below). With her endearing grin and ditsy teenage charm, she landed endorsements worth millions, then turned pro at 15 so she and her folks could lead "a real life."

Tiger WOODS

A prodigal pro wins the Masters at 21

On April 13, 1997, right after he became the Masters' youngest champion (right), the course record holder and the first person of color to win a major tourney, Tiger Woods embraced his dad, Earl (above). After all, it was the Army vet who'd begun teaching his son golf literally before he could walk. (At age 2, Woods putted against Bob Hope on TV— and won.) Dad's efforts have paid off in his boy's awesome swing and ferociously competitive spirit. And the Tiger is still only 23.

LEFT: JAMIE SQUIRE/ALLSPORT; RIGHT: STEVE MUNDAY/ALLSPORT; INSET: DAVE MARTIN/AP

Cameron DIAZ

A beauty who's funny? You got it

She was reluctant, but with persuasion and a brewski or two, the producers of *There's Something About Mary* (1998) got Cameron Diaz, then 25, to use fake sperm as hair gel. And thanks to her dizzying charm, that famous scene made the once-tough Cuban-German-English-Native American kid from Long Beach, California, Hollywood's kooky new darling.

Gwyneth PALTROW

A golden girl lived up to her lineage

Genes told. Gwyneth Paltrow, the willowy blonde from smart showbiz stock (actress Blythe Danner and TV producer Bruce Paltrow) quit college for a crescendoing film career. After a broken romance with Brad Pitt, her big moment arrived (opposite Joseph Fiennes, below) in *Shakespeare in Love*. Paltrow, now 26, portrayed Lady Viola with a grace that in 1999 won over the Academy.

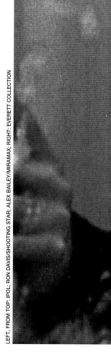

Leonardo DiCAPRIO

For the new king of the world, it has all gone swimmingly

Titanic broke all records (more than $1 billion at the box office) and myriad teen hearts. Leonardo DiCaprio had made waves with his broody, poetic face in *This Boy's Life* and *What's Eating Gilbert Grape* before bobbing to the top with Kate Winslet in 1997. He's dealing with it as most 24-year-old guys would—fielding roles and females, hanging out with his pals, paying visits to sick kids and only occasionally behaving like a brat in public.

Mark McGWIRE

A gentle giant puts baseball back on top

After his record-tying 61st homer on Labor Day 1998, mighty Mark McGwire, 34, swept up his batboy son Matt, 10. There was more to come as dedicated, divorced dad McGwire and equally gracious, Dominican-born Sammy Sosa, 30, homered into history, swatting 70 and 66 respectively, to rejuvenate fan excitement dimmed by an ugly '94 players' strike.

PHIL HARTMAN Over eight seasons, Hartman was a versatile *SNL* staple specializing as Bill Clinton (in '93). He built a career in TV (*NewsRadio*) and movies (*Small Soldiers*) before being murdered by his wife in 1998. He was 49.

CHRIS ROCK He started with idol Eddie Murphy in *Beverly Hills Cop II* and won a major role in *New Jack City* even while performing in *SNL* (with Spike Lee, right, in '91). In 1997 the electrifying 32-year-old got his own show on HBO and late that year hosted MTV's Video Music Awards.

CHRIS FARLEY A Second City alum like Belushi and John Candy, Farley specialized in over-the-top physical comedy. Two years after goofing on Newt Gingrich in Washington, D.C. in 1995, Farley died of a drug overdose at 33.

ADAM SANDLER His loopy parody songs and characters like Cajunman rocketed Sandler, 33 (in '93), to Hollywood. Playing likable losers in *Billy Madison, Happy Gilmore* and *The Waterboy* (a $39-million grosser on its opening weekend) made him a hero to young males. *The Wedding Singer* brought in women.

MIKE MYERS AND DANA CARVEY As slacker teen Wayne Campbell, Myers (with Carvey as sidekick Garth in '91) concocted *Wayne's World,* soon a blockbuster film property. Myers struck again in '97 with the spy spoof *Austin Powers:* and in '99 with its sequel, subtitled *The Spy Who Shagged Me.*

WAYNE'S TOP TEN
1. MADONNA
2. KIM BASINGER
3. GARTH'S MOM
4. HEATHER LOCKLEAR
5. IRENE RYAN
6. FARRAH FAWCETT
7. BETTY RUBBLE
8. JOSEPHINE BAKER
9. ELLE MACPHERSON
10. JULIA ROBERTS

The State of Our
UNIONS

Cruise and Kidman had been wed only five months before going to work on Ron Howard's 1992 Irish epic, *Far and Away*. Perhaps that's why the film's love scenes are so breath-takingly believable.

Celeb romance isn't so different from the civilian sort. There are winners, losers —and many who just keep trying in hopes they'll get it right

1990-

Nicole Kidman & Tom Cruise

Days of Thunder was derided as *Top Gun* with cars instead of planes, but what made this 1990 film memorable was the Cruise-Kidman electricity.

Film's gilded couple plays from strength to strength—and makes it all look easy

Their affair on the Daytona Beach, Florida, set of *Days of Thunder* seemed as lusty and transitory as most location romances. Tom Cruise was just divorced from Mimi Rogers, his wife of three years, and his costar Nicole Kidman was living with a man back home in Australia.

Yet the smitten couple married less than a year later, on Christmas Eve 1990, and their professional and domestic lives have blossomed since. At 37, Cruise has become a successful producer (*Mission: Impossible*) and a mature leading man, with his second Oscar nomination for *Jerry Maguire* (*Born on the Fourth of July* was the first). Kidman, 32, has won respect and raves for her work onscreen (*To Die For*) and onstage (*The Blue Room,* in which she wowed Broadway and London audiences with a brief nude scene). And the pair were chosen by auteur Stanley Kubrick to star in what would be his last film, *Eyes Wide Shut.* They have weathered the media fallout of being a Hollywood golden couple, coping with slurs concerning their faith (Scientology) and their sexuality. Last year, Cruise successfully sued a British tabloid for publishing the rumor that he's gay, that his and Kidman's marriage is a sham.

"The life feeds the work, and the work feeds the life," Cruise once said. Perhaps it's his can-do screen roles that have helped him perform so heroically in a number of real-life accident scenes. Both stars also fall effortlessly and blissfully into their parts as adoptive parents to Isabella, 6, and Connor, 4. "We will be on our honeymoon the rest of our lives," Kidman said in 1992. So far, so good.

"We have so much in common that it's almost as if we are the same person," Kidman has said. "We know what it takes to make each other happy." Evidently son Connor, swinging down an L.A. street in 1998, also knows a thing or two about making Cruise and Kidman happy.

She's only an inch taller than he is, but in heels, Kidman towers over hubby Cruise. At the Golden Globes in 1997, the height difference didn't faze him. In fact, he ate it up.

They met, they loved, they split—and they learned along the way to do the custody duet

The marriage of Billy Joel and Christie Brinkley was one of the original rocker/model unions. She was a pampered, leggy California girl with gleaming teeth and flaxen hair, he a scruffy, blue-collar piano man from Long Island. Joel had weathered a tough divorce from his former manager; Brinkley had been wed to a French illustrator and close to Olivier Chandon de Brialles, a champagne-heir race driver killed in an accident. The couple's nine-year marriage followed his big hit "Uptown Girl" and produced a daughter, Alexa, 13. While separated, Brinkley endured a grisly helicopter accident and, later, a disastrous third marriage. Joel had such severe throat problems he had to cancel tour dates with Elton John. Now things are looking up. Brinkley, 45, seems blissfully happy with her fourth husband, architect Peter Cook. Joel, 50, has an artist girlfriend, Carolyn Beegan, and is realizing his dream of composing classical music. Good friends, Brinkley and Joel live near one other. Both dote on Alexa.

1985-1994

Christie Brinkley & Billy Joel

By 1990, Brinkley and Joel were proud parents and at the top of their commercial games.

After the old stud met the young star, he recalled that 'Everything made sense.' Eight years and three children later, it still does

Warren Beatty & Annette Bening

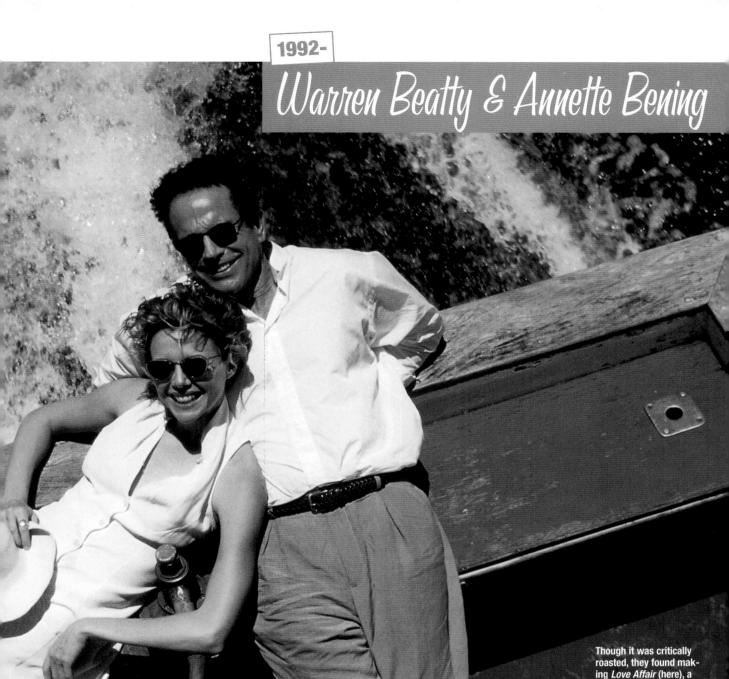

Though it was critically roasted, they found making *Love Affair* (here), a 1994 remake of the classic *An Affair to Remember*, a labor of love.

Warren Beatty's affairs with the likes of Natalie Wood, Julie Christie, Diane Keaton, Isabelle Adjani and Madonna are as much a part of his legend as the talent displayed in a line of distinctive films, including *Bonnie and Clyde* and *Reds* (which won him his only Oscar, for directing). As of 1991 he was still single, Hollywood's leading Lothario. So it was a shock when news came from the set of *Bugsy* that Beatty and his costar Annette Bening were expecting. She was on the cusp of stardom after an Oscar nomination for *The Grifters*—and 21 years younger than Beatty. Doubts about the future and Beatty's settling down were inevitable.

But they wed the following year and, so far, seemingly without regrets. Bening has remarkable energy for a 41-year-old with three children under age 8, and her film career is back on track. She also has ended her 10-year absence from the stage in a much-praised L.A. production of *Hedda Gabler.* Beatty's sister Shirley MacLaine believes that Bening's theater discipline helped the couple: "The show must go on—it's about being there when you said you would. She detected that same trait in Warren." Beatty, who at 62 is riding high on *Bulworth*'s success, sounds serenely at bay. Asked in 1992 about his many lovers, he answered, "I have only one—Annette. I don't remember the others."

"I have never been separated from David for more than two weeks," said Pfeiffer (at a 1996 benefit).

1993–

David E. Kelley & Michelle Pfeiffer

Two of Hollywood's most powerful and private players found joy after a blind date

She was thinking she might never settle down. After a painful 1990 divorce from Peter Horton, Michelle Pfeiffer had dated other actors, including John Malkovich, Fisher Stevens and Michael Keaton. Then, she was 34—and she wanted a baby. She set the adoption wheels in motion, and by the time Claudia arrived, Mom was involved with "this nice, normal TV guy." He was, in fact, the most creative TV guy of the '90s, David E. Kelley, the quiet, Princeton-trained lawyer who conjured up *Picket Fences, The Practice* and, later, *Ally McBeal.* Pfeiffer and Kelley were married the day of Claudia's christening, and, within the week, John Henry was conceived. "My family all sort of came together at once," said Pfeiffer, now 41, so the hardworking actress cut back to accommodate the kids. Kelley, 43, thinks anything she does is fine. Asked if he thought he'd found perfect romantic love, he said, "I do. If anyone came up to me and said, 'There are others out there just like her,' I wouldn't believe it."

For this gracefully graying duo, doing good comes as easily as looking good

Newman wasn't always the bigger star. Woodward won her Academy Award early, in 1957, for *The Three Faces of Eve.* Newman was seventh-time lucky, finally snagging his Best Actor Oscar in '86 for *The Color of Money.* By then, Woodward was mostly caring for the family of six (three from Newman's first marriage) and getting a degree from Sarah Lawrence (she graduated in 1990, alongside daughter Clea). He was the celeb, the heartthrob; on the rare occasions when she chose to act, it was a superb turn, as in 1968's *Rachel, Rachel,* directed by her husband.

The truly impressive thing about them is the dignified, unassuming life they have created. It's in Connecticut—far from Hollywood—and deeply altruistic. There's the Hole in the Wall Gang, a summer camp for kids with terminal illnesses; the antidrug Scott Newman Foundation (named for the son, from his first marriage, who died of an overdose in '78); and Newman's Own, the gourmet food company that now outgrosses his movies, with all profits going to charity. The magnanimity must be in the genes: Two daughters work for philanthropic organizations. Long may they fund-raise.

Married two years in 1960, they were a flirty pair. No wonder he once said, "Joanne's one of the last great broads." According to her, "the only place I'm a sex symbol is at home." They haven't changed much since 1990 (below, left), though Paul is now 74 and Joanne is 69.

1958-

Paul Newman & Joanne Woodward

In 1993, a year before the end, Crawford and Gere dressed down to attend a fashion show in Paris.

1991-1994

Cindy Crawford & Richard Gere

A linkup of a supermodel and 'sexiest man' turned out to be too beautiful to be true

The death knell was perhaps their 1994 full-page ad in *The Times of London* declaring that Richard Gere and Cindy Crawford "are heterosexual and monogamous, and take our commitment to each other very seriously." Ever since eloping in 1991, sealing vows in a Las Vegas chapel with rings of tinfoil, they had fought rumors. Finally, after Gere publicly accused Sylvester Stallone of sleeping with Crawford ("the most bizarre thing I've ever experienced," said Stallone of the accusation), the model sued for divorce. But the marriage was done in not by innuendos but by dueling careers and spiritual beliefs. Gere, now 49, is a devout Buddhist and ambivalent about having kids. Crawford, 33 and pregnant by her second husband, restaurateur Rande Gerber, is a blue-collar midwesterner whose glamorous looks belie a practical character. As photographer Herb Ritts, a friend to each, put it, "Cindy gave it a try, but she's not into eating yak butter."

'Fresh' is the word not only for the Prince he plays but for their match

Back in 1990, Jada Pinkett was rejected for the role of Will Smith's girlfriend on NBC's *The Fresh Prince of Bel-Air.* The producers thought the 5'-tall auditioner was too short for the 6'2" Smith. The producers obviously were mistaken. By 1995, when Smith's first marriage ended, the two actors had become close, and on New Year's Eve 1997, they wed near her native Baltimore. Their son Jaden Christopher Syre was born seven months later.

Smith went from pop success (as half of the rap duo DJ Jazzy Jeff and the Fresh Prince) to prime time to movie superstardom (in the biggest box office hits of 1996 and 1997, *Independence Day* and *Men in Black*). Pinkett's trajectory has been less steep, but after *Scream 2*, she's on her way. From all accounts it's a case of nice guys finishing first. Vivica A. Fox, who has worked with them both, praises Smith as "a one-woman man. He loves being in love and in a relationship." When Debbie Allen hired Pinkett for the sitcom *A Different World,* she told the young actress, "Sweetheart, you got angels on your shoulders."

Maybe they both do. Their love is deep and expressive. For Pinkett's 25th birthday—she's now 27, Smith 30—Smith had an entire truckload of flowers delivered to the movie set where she was shooting. It was a classic Will Smith gesture: generous, affectionate, a bit outrageous—just what *Men in Black*'s casting director David Rubin meant when he said, "It's his ebullience that makes him so irresistible."

"There's nothing I can't share with him," Pinkett has said of Smith— and that includes strutting their stuff at the 1997 premiere of *Metro.*

1997–
Will Smith & Jada Pinkett

In 1997 the Giffords embraced at the Sports Emmy Awards. One month later, after the revelation that rocked their marriage, they withdrew for awhile from public appearances as a couple.

1986–

Frank & Kathie Lee Gifford

When her football-hero spouse fumbled into infidelity, she kept uncommonly mum and stoically forgave the Giffer's gaffe

Bubbly, chatty Kathie Lee Gifford, 45, was the TV hostess America loved—and loved to find irritating—as she blabbed away about her religious faith (she became a born-again Christian at 12), her adorable children Cody and Cassidy, and her adoring husband, sportscaster Frank Gifford, 68, whom she called a "human love machine." But hearts reached out to her in 1997 when a tabloid trapped Frank in a tawdry infidelity. The *Globe* videotaped and made public his liaison in a New York City

hotel room with a flight attendant he had met on a plane. After an initial denial, Frank fessed up and sought penance on *Larry King Live*.

The Giffords had recently dealt with another embarrassment when Kathie Lee's Wal-Mart clothing line was found to have been partially produced in illegal sweatshops, involving child labor. She'd emerged from that crisis with relative dignity and, this time, she kept up her appearances on *Live! with Regis & Kathie Lee* but remained uncharacteristically silent about her woes. (Off-

A social satirist and TV's straightest arrow relish life well beneath the radar

Some public figures prefer to live privately. Take Jane Pauley, a favorite face on TV since her 1976 debut on *Today*. She switched to prime time in 1989 after the younger Deborah Norville began to share the hosts' couch, but many, including Jane's husband, the gonzo *Doonesbury* cartoonist Garry Trudeau, were surprised by her relative lack of outrage. "In Jane's position," he said, "nine out of 10 TV performers would have left tire tracks on Deborah's back." It was a rare press comment by Trudeau, who had once explained, "I've been trying to develop a lifestyle that doesn't require my presence." As for the famously unassuming Pauley, she is pleased that "I'm ordinary looking, so I can walk down a street and not be noticed." Their three kids are also rarely photographed. Behind the blandly pleasant exterior, what is this marriage like? Tom Brokaw confirmed our suspicions: "It's sickeningly perfect."

1980-

Jane Pauley & Garry Trudeau

Even at a movie premiere, like this one in 1997, Pauley, now 48, and Trudeau, 51, dude out like plain folks, not celebrities.

camera she reportedly lashed out, serenading Frank at their joint birthday party with the Eagles' song "Lyin' Eyes.") In private the two set about rebuilding their 12-year marriage (his third, her second). By the end of 1997, when Frank's son-in-law Michael Kennedy (the son of Robert and Ethel Kennedy) was killed in a skiing accident, the Giffords were solidly reconciled. "I think our marriage is much stronger because of what happened," said a rueful Frank. "I don't have her grace. I don't have her strength." And Kathie Lee's former hairdresser concurred: "She's not just some perky little Twinkie. She happens to have some sense."

1987-1998

Bruce Willis & Demi Moore

Scout (left) and Rumer accompanied their parents to the *Striptease* premiere in 1996. "Everything else is stupid compared to having kids," Willis once said.

Danson ended his 1993 roast of Goldberg by eating watermelon. The Friars Club issued a public apology.

A Brat Pack beauty and streetwise action hero lit the sky only to flame out

There was reason to believe the relationship between Demi Moore and Bruce Willis would rock: They were married by Little Richard. Their careers were on the rise. He went on from TV's delightful *Moonlighting* to become a big-time action star in *Die Hard*. She had overcome substance problems to break out in the supernatural weepie *Ghost*. They became the most high-powered celebrity couple of the '90s, playing the role with a gusto that belied their blue-collar roots. He alternated screen blockbusters with artier fare such as *Pulp Fiction*. She posed nude and pregnant for the cover of *Vanity Fair*. They purchased much of the hamlet of Hailey, Idaho, and relocated there. They were highly visible investors in the Planet Hollywood chain, and Willis planned to develop riverfront property he had bought near his New Jersey hometown, Carneys Point. Moore's $12.5 million payday for 1996's *Striptease* made her the highest-paid actress in Hollywood. When she filmed *G.I. Jane* the next year, her entourage required two planes.

They tried to be conscientious parents to their three daughters. But, as a friend said, "they spent too much time away from each other, and they were leading different lives." In 1998, just weeks after winning a lawsuit against a tabloid charge that they were heading for "Hollywood's nastiest divorce in years," they announced their split (the second for Moore, who'd divorced Freddy Moore in '85). Willis, 44, has granted custody of the kids to Moore, 36, and they're working on an amicable division of their estimated assets of $100 million.

1992-1994

Ted Danson & Whoopi Goldberg

Cheers became jeers, and his over-the-top gig at a roast turned their relationship to toast

All that fury caused by their appearance at the 1993 Friar's Club Roast for Whoopi Goldberg was the final blow. They'd been criticized before, ever since they fell in love on the set of *Made in America* and Ted Danson left his wife of 15 years and two children. They were an unlikely couple—he the clean-cut star of *Cheers,* she the twice-married, contentious comic—and they kept a low profile until the roast, when Danson performed a blackface routine so raunchy that some guests protested it as bigotry and walked out. The pair reacted bitterly. Goldberg, now 49, revealed that they had received hate mail from the time they started dating and fulminated, "How can you say, on one hand, that Ted and I are having a relationship— and then call him a racist?" Danson, 51, explained that the material came from the "gallows humor" they used to protect themselves from the public's resentment: "It was brave, you know?" Maybe so, but soon afterward they broke up. Goldberg had a richochet quickie marriage with a union organizer, and then they both settled down with well-regarded actors.

He later wed Mary Steenburgen (with him in 1998); she wound up with Frank Langella (in '99).

The couple made the Hollywood scene (in 1976) but never lived together.

1973-1990

Anjelica Huston & Jack Nicholson

Lovers for years, they seemed to find contentment only after saying *sayonara*

Anjelica Huston met Jack Nicholson in 1973, when he was 36 and already a recognized star and ladies' man. She was 22, living in the shadow of her movie-director father, John. Nicholson reportedly took one look at the hawk-nosed, 5'10" beauty and pronounced her "cla-a-a-ss." Both carried emotional baggage. Huston had watched her gentle ballerina mother treated roughly by John, who had a total of five wives. Nicholson grew up in a house of three women, whom he understood to be his mother and two older sisters—until 1974, when he learned that his so-called mother was his grandmother, and his "sisters" were his mother and his aunt. He already had a child by first wife Sandra Knight, whom he'd divorced in 1968, and another, whom he took years to acknowledge, by Susan Anspach. Small wonder that he and Huston, while deeply loving, did not marry and periodically stepped out (she with Ryan O'Neal, he with many lovers). Finally he conceived a child with Rebecca Broussard, and Huston split. Nicholson is today a besotted father to his two children by the young actress, who lives nearby, and Huston has been married since 1992 to Mexican sculptor Robert Graham.

It took a professional to talk this feminist and onetime foe of wedlock into the bliss they found

When Marlo Thomas appeared on *Donahue* in 1977, the feminist actress had a reputation for walking off shows that she felt invaded her privacy. This time, though, interviewer and interviewee hit it off. "You are a very loving and generous man," Thomas told Phil Donahue. "Whoever is the woman in your life is very lucky."

It was an unlikely remark from the Emmy-winning star of *That Girl,* the trailblazing career-girl sitcom. More typically, Thomas would say, "Marriage is like a vacuum cleaner: You stick it to your ear and, *shhlllurrrppp,* it sucks out all your energy and ambition." The co-creator and star of *Free to Be . . . You and Me* (the record, book and show that told kids they didn't have to live up to anybody's idea of what they should be) was not dying to marry.

Nor was Donahue. His syndicated series was the most successful of its era as well as the most intelligent—a single guest per show, interviewed with journalistic intensity. But success had taken its toll. When he met Thomas, this product of a middle-class, Catholic home in Cleveland was divorced, a single father with custody of his four teenage sons. (His ex-wife retained custody of their daughter.)

Today, Donahue, 63, has finally retired from the now-crasser daytime fray. Thomas, 61, appears as Jennifer Aniston's mother on *Friends* and toils for St. Jude's, the Memphis children's hospital founded by her comedian father, Danny. Their marriage, after almost two decades, is their mission. As Thomas put it, "We are still learning how to live with each other."

"That Girl" settles down: Thomas and Donahue (with Huey and Louie in '95) get away from it all at their Westport, Connecticut, country place.

"I'm the happiest man alive," toasted Kennedy at the rehearsal dinner before his September wedding. The good times seemed to be rolling at this charity fete in June 1996.

69

1996–
JFK Jr. & Carolyn Bessette Kennedy

An artful Calvin Klein aide nabbed the world's most elusive bachelor

He was the catch of the quarter century, the scion of America's royal family and a friendly, outdoorsy, regular guy. Over the years, he'd been linked with a long line of famous beauties, including Brooke Shields, Daryl Hannah and Sarah Jessica Parker. But the woman John wed wasn't a celebrity—they'd met while jogging in Manhattan's Central Park. Was she up to marrying into the Kennedy clan? According to Perry Barlow, a friend of the couple's, "Carolyn's tough, tough as a bobcat."

The reed-slim blonde who once worked as a publicist for Calvin Klein is volatile as well as beautiful. Cameras have caught the couple squabbling, even shoving each other. "You never quite know which way her mood is going to turn," says a friend, "and that makes her quite exciting to be around."

The small wedding in a simple church, built by freed slaves on an island off Georgia, was a masterpiece of secrecy. But the media glare hasn't let up since. Bessette, 33, is rarely seen in public, while Kennedy, 38, busies himself at *George,* the political magazine he cofounded. Meanwhile, the world admires the couple's apparent genetic promise and awaits the next generation of Camelot.

FROM LEFT: CORBIS/DAVID ALLEN; MARCEL THOMAS/SIPA PRESS; TIMOTHY GREENFIELD-SANDERS/OUTLINE

Reeve describes his wife simply: "She is my life force." Judging by this 1996 portrait, the feeling is mutual.

1992–
Christopher Reeve & Dana Morosini

A freak accident felled the rugged star, but the tenacious love of his wife helps him heal

Five days after the 1995 riding accident that left him paralyzed, Christopher Reeve regained enough consciousness to wonder if he'd be better off dead. His wife of three years, actress Dana Morosini, responded, "This is your life and your decision. But I want you to know that I'll be with you for the long haul, no matter what." The going hasn't been easy, but Reeve's resolve has never wavered. The activism that led him to cofound the Creative Coalition, a left-of-center group that also includes Ron Silver, Glenn Close and Susan Sarandon, has turned Reeve into a crusader for the American Paralysis Foundation and his own Christopher Reeve Foundation. In 1997 he made a widely praised directing debut with the HBO movie *In the Gloaming,* and last year he returned to acting in a remake of Hitchcock's *Rear Window.* Best of all for Morosini, 38, Reeve is still here, both as husband and as dad to their son, Will, 7 (Reeve has two other children from a 10-year relationship with Gae Exton). The former caped crusader has vowed that he will walk by his 50th birthday. He's 46 now. Don't bet against Superman.

In 1993 the "hunk that flunked" (his first two bar exams) squired Daryl Hannah.

Hollywood's most prominent gay couple feel unwelcome—but unshaken in their commitment

When Anne Heche, an actress on the fast track, met comedian Ellen DeGeneres at an Oscar party in 1997, their attraction was instant. Heche soon announced, "Ellen and I are very much in a relationship, and we are looking forward to a long future together." DeGeneres had already come out on a TIME cover captioned, "Yep, I'm gay," and in character on her eponymous sitcom. Heche followed after her father, a fundamentalist minister and closeted homosexual, died of AIDS. In the ensuing controversy, Jerry Falwell referred to "Ellen Degenerate," and *Ellen* was canceled. ("I was fired basically because I'm gay," complained DeGeneres; ABC countered that the show had simply stopped being funny). Heche, 30, got a career boost costarring with Harrison Ford in *Six Days, Seven Nights*. And both women continue to get parts but feel non grata and talk about moving out of L.A. "We're just trying to be truthful," said DeGeneres, 41, "and what we've learned is that this is a hard town to be truthful in."

1997-

Anne Heche & Ellen DeGeneres

"I have no fear about this," Heche said of her relationship with DeGeneres (near their home in 1998). "It's the easiest thing in my life I've ever done."

Her newest love, *Law & Order*'s Benjamin Bratt, squired her to a 1998 opening.

Lyle Lovett & Julia Roberts

In 1993 the newly-weds radiated happiness. Today they remain close. "We're the best of friends," said Roberts, "and I can't imagine him not in my life."

The pretty woman and the smart singer tried marriage on for size and found it didn't fit

It was adorable, if odd, while it lasted. Roberts knitted him a sweater; Lovett wrote her some songs. And when the two were out together, they clung and smooched like teenagers. But they weren't together that much, in public or in private. The tremulous, barefoot bride, then 25, and the 35-year-old groom with the ironic, lopsided grin had met only three weeks before their wedding, which was held in a rural church in Marion, Indiana, before a rapidly assembled group of family and friends (such as Susan Sarandon and Tim Robbins). Days later, Roberts was filming again, Lovett was back on tour. She kept her Manhattan apartment, and he stayed in his Texas farmhouse with a dozen relatives nearby. They seemed content to snatch a rendezvous in Paris or on the road. "We're just so happy to be together when we can be," said the inscrutable Lovett. When the marriage ended after 21 months, people wondered why they had bothered. Answer? "They were wonderful together, really in love," said one of Lovett's friends. But, hard workers and independent souls, they underestimated how tough it would be to merge two full lives.

She dumped Kiefer Sutherland four days before their '91 wedding.

In January '98, Hillary (entering church with Bill) called rumors about the White House intern false allegations that had been created by "a vast right-wing conspiracy."

1975-

Bill Clinton & Hillary Rodham Clinton

Celebrating at the 1996 Democratic Convention, the Clintons were already under investigation by Kenneth Starr.

The ultimate power couple have somehow preserved a marriage that critics say betrays her feminist beliefs

In January 1992, Steve Kroft of *60 Minutes* was prodding the Clintons to talk about Bill's alleged affair with Gennifer Flowers. When Kroft praised them for reaching "some sort of an understanding and an arrangement," Bill interrupted. "Wait a minute," he insisted. "You're looking at two people who love each other. This is not an arrangement or an understanding. This is a marriage."

It was what we wanted to hear. It got Bill off the hook and generated the sympathy of millions who recognized their own fallibility in the Clintons' woes. But in the ensuing years, the world has found itself wondering what kind of a marriage this is, when the President, now 53, time and again seems to indulge in reckless dalliances and his resourceful, feminist wife, 51, time and again forgives him. They are well-matched, though she's a Methodist from a solidly midwestern Republican family and he's a southern Baptist from a bumpier Arkansas background. When they met at Yale Law School in 1971, they connected, relishing each other's brilliance, ideology and big ambitions. But it was Bill who went home to run for office and Hillary who turned down a promising Washington, D.C., job to go with him. Three years after their marriage, Bill was elected governor; two years later, their adored Chelsea was born. Ever since, Hillary, as working lawyer and then activist First Lady, has chosen to be Bill's most ferocious supporter, supported in turn by her religious faith and by Chelsea, the center of her emotional life and perhaps the unbreakable bond of the couple's complicated marriage. Through the humiliations concerning Monica Lewinsky (was Hillary the last person in America to know?), impeachment and its aftermath, the couple has grappled with conflicting emotions—and seemed to need each other more than ever.

To help win back the governorship (in '82), she had a makeover and added his surname.

In 1993 they horsed around for a photographer at the Paradise Valley, Montana, ranch where they hike, fish and Jeep around with their brown Lab, Dave.

1991–

Meg Ryan & Dennis Quaid

Funky, hunky and spunky, this duo worked through their difficulties with class

Between the two of them, there's a lot of cute grinning. His grin is sexy and roguish; hers, adorably perky. But there is more to the Meg Ryan-Dennis Quaid union than that. They met on the set of *Innerspace* in 1987 and fell in love on the *D.O.A.* location the following year. Quaid was a cocky show-off. "He courted me relentlessly," recalled Ryan. "I remember thinking, 'Oh, no! Him.'"

As their romance blossomed, the question of his long-standing drug habit came up. It was Ryan's mother, Susan, who first raised the issue, and when she told Meg, it resulted in a bitter estrangement between mother and daughter that still persists. (There had been big trouble earlier, when Meg was just a teenager and her mom walked out on her marriage and into a new life, leaving the four children with Dad.) When Quaid later acknowledged his cocaine problem, Ryan refused to marry him until he'd gone into rehab, whereupon he changed his fast-living ways and embarked on some serious soul-searching. That sea change made their 1991 marriage possible.

Friends find the couple's relationship inspiring. "They have a very strong bond," says director Griffin Dunne, "I sense that they've been through a lot together." Both of their careers are flourishing, but their primary joy is 7-year-old Jack Henry Quaid. Remembering the pain of her own childhood, Ryan is a hands-on mom. "I'm his parent," she has said. "I'm supposed to take care of him." She often picks him up from school, Quaid coaches his soccer team, and all three regularly indulge in wild, vicious Super Soaker games on their front lawn in Santa Monica or at their sprawling Montana spread. As Quaid put it last year, "There's always going to be another movie, but Jack's never going to be 6 again."

Last fall, Schiffer cuddled with her fiancé between acts while he was performing in her native Germany.

1994- Claudia Schiffer & David Copperfield

They're well-matched, good-looking and loaded, but Houdini-esque in eluding the altar

Three months after they met at a gala where he was performing, magician David Copperfield placed a 5-carat diamond ring on the finger of supermodel Claudia Schiffer. But that presto occurred way back in January 1994, and there's been no change-o since in their status. Officially the word is that their hectic schedules are keeping them apart. Unofficially, well, nobody has dared to speculate since Copperfield sued *Paris Match* for $30 million after the magazine claimed he'd hired Schiffer to act as his fiancée. At a Milan fashion show last fall, Schiffer insisted, "Of course I'll get married," but didn't say when. Another time she told reporters, "I'd really like to change my life." That's hardly surprising. After all, she's 28, which is matronly for a model, and is no longer involved with the floundering Fashion Café. David Kotkin (as he was born 42 years ago in Metuchen, New Jersey) said through his spokeswoman last year that he and Schiffer "are still very much engaged but still don't have a wedding date."

This placid 1991 portrait aside, the earth mother of 14 found in him a kid she couldn't handle.

1980-1992

Woody Allen & Mia Farrow

Her TV *Peyton Place* was peanuts compared to their long-running, sordid-ending love affair

They were an odd couple. Mia Farrow, a Hollywood legacy, was as famous for failed marriages (to Frank Sinatra and Andre Previn) as for career successes. Woody Allen grew up in Brooklyn and sold jokes while in high school. His two marriages (one to Louise Lasser) and affair with Diane Keaton took a backseat to his relentless productivity. But the pair clicked, waving to each other through binoculars from their apartments on opposite sides of Manhattan's Central Park. They never married but by 1992 had made 13 movies together, produced one child (Satchel, now 11) and adopted two others (Moses, 21, and Dylan, 14). Then Farrow

Soon-Yi Previn was 20 when she joined Allen at this '90 Knicks game.

found nude pictures of her adopted daughter Soon-Yi Previn on Allen's mantel. All hell broke loose. She accused him of sexually abusing daughter Dylan. He sued Farrow for custody of their children. She won, but the bad blood still flows. Farrow, now 54, detailed Allen's neurotic behavior in her memoir; he blasted her "compulsive" adopting. Allen and Previn wed in 1997, and this year they got a daughter of their own.

It seems like she will always love him, but he knows how to test a girl

He's not the kind of date you rush to bring home to Mom —especially if Mom is Cissy Houston, a veteran soul singer and devout Baptist from Newark, New Jersey, and the guy in question is a bad-tempered boozer with three children by two different women. Nonetheless, Whitney Houston began dating R&B singer Bobby Brown in 1991 and married him the following summer before 800 guests at her New Jersey mansion. Eight years later he's 32, she's 36, and they're still together, with a 6-year-old daughter, Bobbi Kristina.

It has been a predictably bumpy ride. By the time they met, Houston, a choir girl from age 8, was a major pop diva and just a few years from breaking into movie stardom with *The Bodyguard.* Brown, a big hit with his single "Don't Be Cruel," was headed toward a career slump, exacerbated by his misbehavior—public drunkenness, womanizing and assorted public scuffles. Over the years the pair have had to handle ugly rumors about their relationship and acknowledge their "marital difficulties" amid reports of screaming fights and separations. But they've seemed determined to stick it out. "He takes care of me,"says Houston. "I don't have to be scared of anything because I know he will kick every ass." Her friends aren't surprised at that rough talk, noting that Houston too has a wild streak and is known for being late for shows (even for Nelson Mandela) and sassing interviewers. As for the incorrigible Brown, he turned himself in last fall to serve a five-day jail sentence for driving while intoxicated.

"We vowed to do it forever . . . to fight hard and to love hard, and to fight hard for the love," says Houston (with Brown at the *Cinderella* premiere in 1997).

1992-

Whitney Houston & Bobby Brown

1979-1997

Farrah Fawcett & Ryan O'Neal

His movie with ex-love Streisand was called *The Main Event,* but it was just a prelim to his long, rocky love match that followed

Majors married Fawcett in '73 and wanted dinner on the table at 6:30 during their six-year union.

She had jiggled her way to fame as the blondest of Charlie's Angels— the U. of Texas beauty queen with the hairdo, who sold 12 million posters and wed the Six Million Dollar Man, a comparably big TV male of the '70s. Farrah Fawcett had even hyphenated Lee Majors's surname onto her own, but the marriage was doomed when he introduced her to old pal Ryan O'Neal in 1979. O'Neal's romantic legend (which included Barbra Streisand, Diana Ross and a couple of failed marriages producing three chil-

dren) exceeded his screen legacy, though he won an Oscar nomination for 1970's *Love Story.* Fawcett and O'Neal made a golden couple. Sue Mengers, onetime agent to both, recalled how "they'd walk into the room like two beautiful Barbie dolls and take your breath away."

But while her career hit new peaks, his was a veritable valley of the dogs. Critics admired her powerful portrayals in *Extremities* and *The Burning Bed.* He blamed his off-type casting in Stanley Kubrick's period drama *Barry Lyndon,* maintaining, "I never got a good job

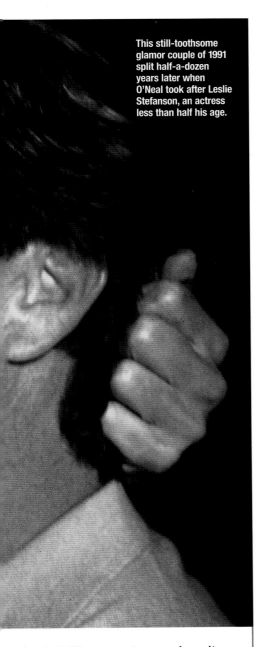

This still-toothsome glamor couple of 1991 split half-a-dozen years later when O'Neal took after Leslie Stefanson, an actress less than half his age.

Of all her marriages, including two to Burton, No. 8 was least likely to succeed

She has always believed in love, and in 1988, at 56, she found it yet again at California's Betty Ford Center, where she and Larry Fortensky, a construction worker 20 years her junior, had gone to get clean. The quiet, 10th-grade dropout got a taste of his life change when they wed (she was his third spouse, he her seventh) at Neverland, Michael Jackson's ranch, under a sky aroar with media choppers. Taylor tried to pare down the star trappings, even donning an apron to fuss around the kitchen. But it was still her world, and Fortensky, having quit his old job, never felt quite at home. The degree of his bitterness became public when Taylor filed for divorce and he counter-filed for spousal support, saying she had "completely changed" his lifestyle, necessitating, for example, $850 monthly dry-cleaning bills for his new designer outfits. It was a far cry from the Mike Todd and Richard Burton days, but Taylor didn't harbor a grudge; and when Fortensky fell over a condo railing and lapsed into a coma this year, she phoned him at the hospital. As she explained, "If I love somebody, I love them always."

1991-1996

Liz Taylor & Larry Fortensky

Taylor's three painful hip operations made life difficult for the couple (in 1992).

after it." His reputation as a brawling hothead didn't help after he knocked out son Griffin's teeth in a 1983 row. O'Neal and Fawcett together had a son, Redmond, in 1985, and costarred in a 1991 sitcom, *Good Sports,* which bombed on CBS. They finally split in '97 without ever having married.

Fawcett, now 52, earned fine reviews in *The Apostle* but received more attention for her nude video, her discombobulated appearance on *Letterman* and the beatings that she allegedly had received from producer-director boyfriend James Orr. O'Neal, 58, who has resurfaced in a few films, said last year, "My career's in the hands of the gods."

"My family is the reason I live, not the work," says Fox (hugging Pollan in '98). They met while making *Family Ties* but didn't get together until years later.

1988–
Michael J. Fox & Tracy Pollan

A dire diagnosis only tightened the family ties of a determined couple

When Michael J. Fox disclosed last fall that he was suffering from Parkinson's disease, he had been struggling with its effects for seven years. Ironically an affliction associated with old age struck a man so boyish that, at 38, Fox still calls to mind the junior yuppie of *Family Ties* or Marty McFly of the *Back to the Future* trilogy. Offstage, though, he is very much the grown-up and family man. He and Tracy Pollan, 39, who costarred with him on *Family Ties,* have a 10-year-old son and 4-year-old twin girls. For their sakes, Fox made some mature choices: He gave up playing ice hockey, the native Canadian's lifelong passion, before he had to. And he opted for the regularity of a TV series, *Spin City,* shooting in New York City, Pollan's hometown. When they can, the family escapes to their Vermont farm.

Last spring, Fox underwent a thalamotomy, a procedure that he hopes will control his tremors and spasms. He is determinedly optimistic that a cure for Parkinson's will emerge. "He's truly remarkable," says Pollan. "He lives today. He lives the moment. And the moment is good."

On their 1994 Hungarian honeymoon, the two visited a children's hospital and handed out toys.

FROM LEFT: MICHAEL O'NEILL/OUTLINE; SCREEN SCENES: KEN GOFF/GLOBE PHOTOS

1994-1996
Lisa Marie Presley & Michael Jackson

They got together for what they shared— a public youth—but couldn't cut it in private

The groom chewed gum throughout the 15-minute ceremony in the Dominican Republic. And the couple was accompanied on their Budapest honeymoon by 47 friends, a PR team, five bodyguards, a film crew, a dance troupe, 2,655 soft toys and a dwarf named Misha. The press called the marriage a sham: Lisa Marie Presley just wanted to entice him into her faith (Scientology), Michael Jackson sought a cover-up for his child-molestation charges. But Jackson, now 41, and Presley, 31, did have something in common. They'd known each other since she was a kid and Elvis would take her to see the Jackson Five. Over the years they'd stayed close, through her six-year marriage to musician Danny Keough and Jackson's legal and drug problems. What drove them apart was living together, though they barely did. While they presented a unified front in public, Presley refused to move to Neverland and reportedly hated Jackson's indulgent parenting of her two kids. After 20 months she walked, and he found a new wife, his dermatologist's assistant Debbie Rowe, who provided him with two children of his own.

1990-?

Mick Jagger & Jerry Hall

In 1982, four months before this happy clinch, Jagger strayed, and Hall brought him to heel by instigating a quickie romance with a British horse breeder.

Jumpin' Jack Flash finally learns that even he can't always get what he wants

Not even his most devoted fan would claim that Mick Jagger is a gentleman song-ster. Throughout the Rolling Stones' extended midnight ramble, he has been the embodiment of decadent, preening sexuality, conducting highly public affairs with, among others, Marianne Faithfull and Marsha Hunt, and enjoying flings with several generations of willowy models. There was also a nine-year marriage to Bianca Perez Morena that produced daughter Jade.

But in 1977 he seemed to have met his mannequin match in Jerry Hall, now 43 and his wife since 1990. The long, tall Texan responded to Mick's dalliances with her own. And in 1992, when he left her bedside after the birth of the third of their four children to canoodle with model Carla Bruni in Thailand, Hall threatened divorce. Jagger returned and they made up, though, as Hall has said, "I always hoped that one day he would outgrow these things."

He hasn't. Last November, Jagger was photographed leaving Bruni's Paris apartment. The next day, rumors surfaced that Brazilian model Luciana Morad was carrying his baby. Hall moved out and hired the attorneys who had handled Princess Diana's divorce. When she sought $50 million, twice the Charles-Di settlement, Jagger countered that his Bali wedding to Hall had never been legal. "I think the public perception of Mick Jagger," noted one London editor, "is that he's a bit of an arse, and a greedy one at that." The consensus was that a rock god of 56 should not delegitimize his children to save a few quid.

By 1982, Reynolds was wooing Anderson with lavish gifts, including a green Rolls Royce.

FROM LEFT: NORMA PARKINSON/CAMERA PRESS/RETNA LTD.; VISAGES

1988-1994

Loni Anderson & Burt Reynolds

He followed legendary relationships with Dinah and Sally with a marriage that became WW III

In a split you wouldn't wish on your worst enemy, Burt Reynolds left his Florida home one night in 1993, telling Loni Anderson, his wife of five years, that he needed time alone. "You're the love of my life, kid," were his departing words. The next morning, Anderson awoke to find news helicopters hovering overhead, a lawyer at the door with a plane ticket to L.A. and two sheriffs bearing divorce papers. The subsequent battle broke new ground in ugliness. He blasted her on TV. Each trashed the other in print: Her book detailed his violence, infidelity and drug addiction; his accused her of infidelity and of being a bad mother to their adopted son, Quinton.

Anderson, now 54, pulled her life back together, buoyed by Quinton and daughter Deidra (from a teen marriage) and an occasional film role. For Reynolds, 63, it got worse. In 1996 the former lover of such celebrated women as (first wife) Judy Carne, Dinah Shore and Sally Field filed for bankruptcy. But the success of 1997's *Boogie Nights* generated new work and an outlook that made it possible for the couple to declare peace.

He (in 1996) admitted to "rough spots" in collaborating on *Dead Men Walking*—"but we got through it. We're still together."

1988–

Susan Sarandon & Tim Robbins

They're not married nor likely to be. But that's the least interesting thing about them

When Barbara Walters asked that endlessly recurring question, Sarandon responded, "Why don't I marry him? I had forgotten that we didn't. There's so much children and real estate." Sarandon, 52, and Tim Robbins, 40, have two sons at home, Jack Henry and Miles, plus Eva, Sarandon's daughter from an earlier relationship. (She also was wed to actor Chris Sarandon from 1967-79.) As for property, they own a New York City brownstone and a home in the suburbs. They share serious careers and deep commitment to their causes and to each other. *Bull Durham* brought them together in 1988, launching the sexy-older-woman phase of Sarandon's filmography. She won an Oscar for 1995's *Dead Man Walking* (Robbins was nominated as director of the picture). They had stirred controversy at the Awards three years earlier, when she spoke out for Haitian refugees with AIDS. But as the passionate Sarandon argues, "How can you not participate in the world you live in?"

A much-married wild child settles down at last with her mucho Latin lover

Destiny brought us together," said Melanie Griffith breathily in 1995, when she and Antonio Banderas went public with their romance. Destiny, of course, can be a corkscrew road. At 15, Griffith had moved in with the seven-years-older Don Johnson. By 19, having briefly wed and divorced him, she was playing sluts and nuts in films that required little in the way of acting or wardrobe. When Griffith was hit by a car at 23 while crossing Sunset Boulevard, she called it "God's way of telling me to slow down" her hard-drinking, druggy life. Fifteen years later, when she met Banderas, a classically trained Spanish actor who had come to the U.S. to costar with her (though he spoke no English at the time), she'd had two more marriages and two children. She had also grown into a real actress.

Shooting *Two Much* together, they were soon necking between takes. "We were totally overwhelmed," recalled Banderas, "and unable to be without each other." That required some rearranging, since both had spouses then. By the time they were clear to wed, Griffith was already pregnant with their daughter Stella del Carmen. Today, Griffith, 42, and Banderas, 39, live in L.A. and plan to have more kids. Said she: "I used to dream about this kind of love when I was little."

Griffith and Don Johnson were married twice, in 1976 and again in '89.

After three years of marriage, the couple still could not keep their hands off each other at the 1999 Golden Globe Awards.

1996-

Melanie Griffith & Antonio Banderas

Roseanne insisted that the seven-years-younger Arnold get his drug habit under control before they married. He did and they did in 1990.

1990-1994

Roseanne & Tom Arnold

The queue of dysfunction and her second banana made an ideal match—while it lasted

They yocked and shocked around the clock. At a 1989 World Series game, they dropped their drawers to display tattooed behinds. Their brief, noisy union followed Roseanne's courageous escape from her tenement youth and embodied her raucous "domestic goddess" role on TV. They'd met in 1983 on the stand-up circuit, and five years later Roseanne hired Tom Arnold as a writer and warm-up act for her TV show. "He's the one person who has ever kept up with me," said Roseanne, and they settled down with her three kids from her first marriage. They chattered constantly to an avid press about their addictions, sex lives, body-image problems and recovered memories of sexual abuse. They even announced plans to jointly "marry" Arnold's pert 24-year-old assistant. In 1994, Roseanne filed for divorce, alleging spousal abuse. She wed her bodyguard Ben Thomas, had another child and divorced last year at 45. Arnold's rebound marriage also tanked.

A diva turned filmmaker found a new dawn at twilight with a TV dude

This was unmistakably a Streisand production, organized down to the last detail— the 4,000 roses, the 16-piece orchestra conducted by Marvin Hamlisch, the 18th-century porcelain plates and, at the center of it all, Barbra herself, not merely marrying handsome, silver-haired James Brolin but also singing two songs composed for the occasion. The reviews were great. "It was probably the most beautiful wedding I've been to," said John Travolta.

The beauty went beyond the lavish appointments. Streisand had been slowly learning to accept the fact that, with her marriage to Elliott Gould over in 1971 and a long list of fizzled romances, from Jon Peters to Don Johnson, behind her, she might never find another love. Brolin, two years older at 59, was that Hollywood rarity, a man she couldn't intimidate. After two long marriages and three children, he was mellow. Knowing little about each other's career and caring less, they embarked on a joyful, down-to-earth love affair. Completely confident, he had proposed several times before she finally said yes. Brolin secretly hoped for a drive-through Vegas ceremony but affably acquiesced to Streisand's grander plans. She'd "never had a real wedding before," said a friend, "and Jim encouraged it."

She celebrated with him (here and below, left) in 1998, when Brolin too got a star on the Hollywood Walk of Fame. He had moved in with her two years earlier, shortly after they met.

1998-

Barbra Streisand & James Brolin

MORTAL

Some Deaths
Don't Just
Make Us Sad,
They Make Us
Question the
Meaning of
Life Itself

SHOCKS

PRINCESS Diana

AUGUST 31, 1997 Her brief life brought a new springtime to the winter of the Windsors, and in the heartbreak over her loss, the whole world showered her with bouquets

Di was happy again. A year after her painful divorce from Prince Charles, she had seemingly surmounted her ailments and problems, walked away from some ill-chosen boyfriends and found a new sense of purpose. She had gone bravely back on the road for her causes. She had helped her boys adjust to the sundering of the family. And then, there was her romance with jet-setting Dodi Fayed, 42, son of the Egyptian-born billionaire Mohammed Al Fayed. For weeks, Dodi and a radiant Di had been all over the French Riviera, lounging and tanning on the beaches, tantalizing the ubiquitous paparazzi. On one particular evening, the two were in Paris, nesting in the luxurious, Al Fayed-owned Ritz Hotel. Before heading out for dinner, Di called her favorite London journalist, Richard Kay of *The Daily Mail,* to confide that she was planning to cut back on public appearances and concentrate on her burgeoning private life. Reporters knew Di's fondness for dramatic pronouncements, but Kay believed her this time. "All was well with her world," he later recounted sadly.

The photographers were being particularly oppressive, so the couple ate in the hotel and then decided to return to Dodi's apartment in a black Mercedes, with Henri Paul driving and Trevor Rees-Jones, Dodi's bodyguard, beside him. The 90-mph crash in the tunnel beside the Place de L'Alma left Fayed and Paul dead, Diana mortally injured and Rees-Jones with no memory of what had happened.

Tony Blair, Britain's prime minister, tried to speak for everyone who felt that in losing this beautiful, beguiling woman in the prime of her life, they had lost a dear member of their own family. With a trembling voice and tears in his eyes, he called her "the People's Princess." The title stuck, through the weeks that followed, as millions of people across the world grieved for their princess. "I think the biggest disease this world suffers from in this day and age is the disease of people feeling unloved," declared Diana, herself the child of a nasty divorce and the survivor of a cold marriage. "I know I can give love." She was right—and in her too-short 36 years, she proved it.

In 1997, Diana crusaded for land-mine victims in Angola and Bosnia, and for AIDS sufferers in South Africa.

She cavorted with William at the Al Fayed family villa near Saint-Tropez in '97. Harry was also along on their last vacation together.

Diana's brother Earl Spencer, her sons and her ex-husband, Prince Charles, bowed in salute as her casket left Westminster Abbey.

ELVIS
PRESLEY

AUG. 16, 1977 The King was dead before his time—after a too-short, unhappy prime

Priscilla Beaulieu was a 14-year-old Air Force brat when Presley met her in Germany. She moved in with him at 17, married him at 21 and split at 28, four years after they posed for this royal portrait in Beverly Hills in 1969.

I t seems to be a continuing battle against mortality, and Elvis is not winning," said rock critic Peter Guralnick in 1976, the year before Presley died at 42, a bloated and drug-addicted wreck. The polite young man from Tupelo, Mississippi, with the devilish grin and the moves to go with it, had, in the '50s, helped change the world, melding blues, country and gospel into rock and roll. Mobbed by adoring teenagers, decried as a corrupter of America's youth, he was in fact a homebody who loved his mom, Gladys, didn't drink, and, when the Army called, submitted to the draft. He also submitted to Col. Tom Parker, who masterminded his career from the raunchy, rowdy heyday of *Heartbreak Hotel* (1956) through the surging, full-voiced ballad phase of *Are You Lonesome Tonight?* (1960) and the string of good-grossing if tepid movies. Basically a shy loner, he never learned how to handle fame. When his six-year marriage collapsed, wife Priscilla took little Lisa Marie to California. That left Elvis bouncing around the walls of his garish Graceland estate in Memphis, surrounded by what we would now call enablers, who supplied him with a cornucopia of junk food and drugs. He still sold racks of records (the total exceeds a billion), and loyal female hordes packed his embarrassing Las Vegas gigs, coveting his sweat-soaked scarves. As Ken Brixey, a Graceland Enterprises marketer, summed it up: "He was a blue-collar worker who, in spirit, never tried to rise above his roots. He is the epitome of a man who started out with nothing, became something and never lost his attraction to the masses. He's a true folk hero."

In 1977, Elvis still filled houses and, alas, his costumes. He suffered from diabetes, hypertension and an enlarged colon as well as obesity.

Jonestown

Jones's Peoples Temple followers had rehearsed, many times, drinking the grape-flavored "poison." This time, the poison was for real.

To 913 disciples he was 'Father' and, in the end, executioner

They started with the babies, doling out Kool-Aid mixed with cyanide. The potion did its work in five excruciating minutes. By the end, 914 men, women and children were dead, the layers of bodies bloating under the scorching Guyanan sun. Cult leader Jim Jones, 47, and his guards were the last to go, by gunshot. As word filtered out, it became clear that this horror had been inevitable. Jones, a cunning, charismatic political player from San Francisco, had established his "Christian socialist" commune in the South American rain forest in 1974, recruiting mostly working-class blacks from the Bay Area. As Jones turned into a paranoid, drug-addicted dictator, his commune became a concentration camp. Prompted by relatives' complaints, California Congressman Leo J. Ryan went to investigate but was killed on the airport tarmac. Knowing it was over, Jones screamed to his followers that they would "meet in another place," and the slaughter began.

John Lennon was a Liverpudlian who came to love Manhattan. "I can go out right now and go into a restaurant. People will ask for autographs, but they won't bug you," he told a BBC interviewer just two days before he was murdered in front of his apartment building, the Dakota. The killer, a 25-year-old drifter named Mark David Chapman, was observed getting Lennon's signature on an album jacket a few hours before the shooting. But the cruelest irony is that Lennon was struck down as he was returning to the spotlight he'd avoided for five years.

His retreat was precisely the kind of unexpected and dramatic gesture we had come to count on from the most brilliant and iconoclastic of the Fab Four, the Beatle who had said they were more popular than Jesus and told the audience at their Royal Command Performance to "rattle your jewelry." His 1969 marriage to avant-gardist Yoko Ono was widely believed to have precipitated the breakup of history's most beloved pop group. Then, in 1975, after an occasional hit single and eight unevenly received albums in his inevitably anticlimactic solo career, Lennon decided to "get as far away from the music business as I could." Yoko took charge of their financial dealings while John became a househusband, taking primary responsibility for the couple's newborn son, Sean. For five years, Lennon baked bread, played games, changed diapers. It was not a sacrifice, he insisted, explaining, "Sean is my biggest pride."

The day after the murder, thousands of Lennon's fellow New Yorkers gathered in Central Park, near the Dakota, to grieve silently for a musical genius whose smart, cantankerous nature had made him the voice of his generation.

JOHN Lennon

DEC. 8, 1980 A virtuoso is a victim of a crazed age that he wryly appreciated and hymned

"Everything I know, Yoko taught me," Lennon proudly told a reporter. "She is my wife, my lover, my friend." A month before his murder, the couple posed (in a Manhattan art gallery) for this serene portrait.

PRINCESS
Grace

SEPT. 14, 1982 From Hollywood to the Riviera, a Philly filly became royalty

Periodically rumors would surface that Princess Grace of Monaco was about to make an acting comeback. But, as her *High Noon* co-star Gary Cooper wondered, "Why would she? She's moved from an artificial stage to a real one." Grace Kelly had appeared in only 11 movies over five years (including *Rear Window, High*

Society, To Catch a Thief and her Oscar-winning *Country Girl*) when she married Prince Rainier in 1956.

A coolly elegant beauty from Philadelphia, Grace wasn't born to the nobility—her father had been an Irish emigré bricklayer before making his fortune—but for 26 years, in Monaco, she was supremely regal, spending long days at her duties and helping her

beloved, if sometimes exasperating, children handle their high-profile lives. She sent the shy Albert away to college at Amherst, acquiesced in Caroline's brief, disastrous marriage to playboy Philippe Junot and stoically waited for Stephanie to grow out of her rebellious ways. "I think of myself as a modern, contemporary woman who has had to deal with all kinds of problems that

Grace (visiting with orphans in 1962) was Diana-like in her devotion to causes such as the Red Cross and Monaco's Princess Grace Ballet School.

A serious blues fan, Belushi created, with Dan Aykroyd, The Blues Brothers—to perform with musicians they idolized and (as at this event in 1980) to party hard with them as well.

many women today have to deal with," Grace once said.

It was a then only 17-year-old Stephanie who was riding with her mother on a winding mountain road back to Monte Carlo when Grace suffered a cerebral hemorrhage. She lost control of the car, which plunged down a 45-foot embankment. Stephanie was bruised; Grace died of her injuries, at 52.

JOHN Belushi

MARCH 5, 1982

The excesses that suffused his comedy ultimately destroyed him

There was no reason for surprise when John Belushi turned up dead in a Los Angeles hotel bungalow with cocaine and heroin in his veins. "The same violent urge that makes John great will ultimately destroy him," predicted *SNL* writer Michael O'Donoghue a few years earlier. Belushi was as excessive, explosive and incorrigible off-camera as on. The son of Albanian immigrants and a onetime homecoming king of Illinois' Wheaton Central High (where he met his wife, Judith), he was America's favorite drug-crazed lunatic. Dick Ebersol, once *SNL*'s producer, said of the original cast, "Belushi was the first to become the audience's friend." The characters he left behind included the bacchanal frat boy Bluto, the Samurai dry-cleaner and the Greek-diner guy. He dined with Robert De Niro the night he died and agreed to lose 40 pounds to get in shape for a role in *Once Upon a Time in America.* "Go out onstage like a bull in a bullring," Belushi had advised his younger brother Jim. It was a credo he himself lived and died by, at 33.

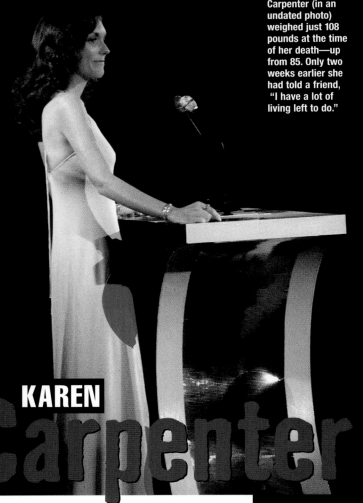

Carpenter (in an undated photo) weighed just 108 pounds at the time of her death—up from 85. Only two weeks earlier she had told a friend, "I have a lot of living left to do."

KAREN Carpenter

FEB. 4, 1983
She was pop music's girl next door—until she starved herself to death

In 1973, when the Carpenters performed at the White House, Richard Nixon introduced them as "young America at its very best." Connecticut-born Californians, Richard and Karen Carpenter were always an anomaly in the pop-music world, a brother and sister duo as colossally uncool as they were successful. They performed airy, mid-tempo love songs in arrangements (by Richard) that built layer upon layer of schmaltzy strings and vocal harmonies around Karen's lilting alto (and her own backing on drums). Rock fans dismissed them, but they sold 30 million records.

By 1983, their heyday was history; and Karen's anorexia, which she'd been battling for almost a decade, was proving intractable. Meanwhile her first solo album, a deliberate effort to escape her white-bread image, was withdrawn from release. An attempted reunion album with her brother never made it out of the studio. Her 1980 marriage had fizzled after 14 months. One morning, at age 32, Karen collapsed in a bedroom of her parents' house and died less than an hour later. It was not the ending that one would have anticipated for the cleanest-cut vocalist of her time.

OCT. 23, 1983 On a Sunday morning, 241 sleepy troops made the ultimate sacrifice

A Marine was fetching a drink of water outside the Marine Corps Barracks in Lebanon, more commonly known as the Beirut Hilton. Suddenly he saw a red Mercedes truck come bursting through the building's iron main gate. "Oh, God, a car bomb," he thought. After swerving around a sandbag barricade and smashing through a flimsy sentry box, the truck drove straight into the building and halted in the lobby. The driver had been smiling on his way in, according to a witness. Now he detonated the 2,500-pound bomb he was carrying, and in seconds the four-story building collapsed around him, killing scores of soldiers as they lay in bed and crushing many more. The blast was so powerful that bodies were hurled 50 feet away. "I haven't seen carnage like that since I was in Vietnam," said Maj. Robert Jordan, a Marine spokesman.

Because many of the soldiers were not wearing their dog tags as they slept and all personnel records were destroyed in the fireball, relatives of the young victims had to wait agonizing days for definite word. For too many families, it came in the shape of a ramrod-straight Marine in uniform ringing the front doorbell to deliver the unthinkable news in person. Though impeccably trained and at their physical peak, the Marines in Lebanon had been helpless against the determination of one suicide-bomber. The average age of those who died was 20.

THE
Marine Barracks

Miraculously there were survivors. Rescue teams of Marines and Lebanese and Italian soldiers labored day and night to dig them out of the smoking rubble.

"Obviously a major malfunction" were the first cryptic words the NASA technician spoke over the Kennedy Space Center public-address system about the horrifying sight that had just unfolded above the spectators, among them relatives of the crew. The *Challenger* lifted smoothly off the pad and rose majestically into the blue Florida sky. Then, without warning, it was enveloped by a massive orange fireball and blew apart. The pieces fell back to earth from nine miles up, trailing plumes of white smoke and a great many questions. But first there were victims to mourn, seven individuals whose lives and families we would come to know well in the days following the disaster.

The crew was a gloriously American mosaic—male, female, black, white, Japanese-American, Catholic, Jewish, Protestant—but none made a larger impression than the mission's sole civilian, a New Hampshire high school teacher named Christa McAuliffe, 37. For all her training, she refused to call herself an astronaut, preferring to say she was merely a "space participant." Yet she was the first of her profession in space, a responsibility she took very seriously. "I touch the future. I teach," she once told an audience. She'd brought her son's toy frog onboard, and she planned to teach a couple of classes from the capsule. But, most of all, she looked forward to returning home to her students, her husband, Steven, and the two kids—Scott, then 9, and Caroline, 6—she missed tucking into bed at night.

In time, we would learn about the failure of the O-ring seals that had caused the catastrophe. The first fatality since three crewmen had died on the pad 19 years earlier reminded us of the perils of space and the bravery of our astronauts.

JAN. 28, 1986 Only 73 seconds into an historic flight, the space shuttle exploded

THE Challenger

Christa McAuliffe (above, second from right, flanked by Michael Smith, left, back-up crew member Barbara Morgan and Francis Scobee) strode toward the *Challenger* months before the tragic flight. In the stands at launch (below, left) were Christa's mom and dad, Grace and Ed Corrigan (in cap) and (in front of them) her sister Lisa.

By 1980, Gilda was no longer the gangly girl of *Saturday Night Live,* but a composed and dignified woman.

GILDA
Radner

A beloved comedienne left a dual legacy of laughter and caring

My life had made me funny, and cancer wasn't going to change that," Gilda Radner wrote in her autobiography *It's Always Something*. It never did. Husband Gene Wilder recalled her shouting at the cancer racing through her body in the wiseacre voice of Roseanne Roseannadanna, "Hey, what are you trying to do here? Make me sick?" When her hair fell out (usually, she joked, into the food when dining with friends), her preferred covering was a cheesy, clownish wig.

Radner's gift for comedy was greater than her gift for happiness. Growing up near Detroit in comfortable circumstances, she lost her father at 14 and developed the obsessive concern about her weight that would dog her through life. On the strength of such talents as her ability to play 14 Bingo cards at once or to recite, on the spot, everything she'd eaten that day, Radner was the first woman hired for *Saturday Night Live*. In a male-dominated show she was an instant hit, not only funny but incredibly sweet. "You felt like you knew her," said Alan Zweibel, another *SNL* writer. "She was a star, but she was your sister." Radner attributed her popularity to "saying yes to every kid on a high school newspaper who called for an interview."

After a short-lived marriage to *SNL* guitarist G.E. Smith and a battle with bulimia, she fell in love with Gene Wilder on the set of their film *Hanky Panky*. They married in 1984, and within 18 months, Radner began to experience pains, flu-like symptoms and fever. She was told her aches were imaginary. By the time the ovarian malignancy was found, it was too late. Not that she didn't fight, undergoing nine rounds of chemo and 30 radiation treatments in the two-and-a-half years before her death at 42. Inspired by her suffering and her strength, Wilder and Radner's psychotherapist Joanna Bull created Gilda's Clubs, retreats where cancer patients and their families can unwind, cry, laugh, be themselves. "Once again," says Radner's brother Michael, "Gilda is making people happy."

As Roseanne Roseannadana (in 1978), she aired hilariously strong views on earwax, hair on soap in people's homes and other unmentionable topics.

Her Emily Litella (in 1979) had an ax to grind in a polite but dogged way. She stayed polite when she turned out to be wrong, which was always.

When Gilda linked romantically with Gene Wilder on their film shoot (in 1981), she said, "My life went from black-and-white to Technicolor."

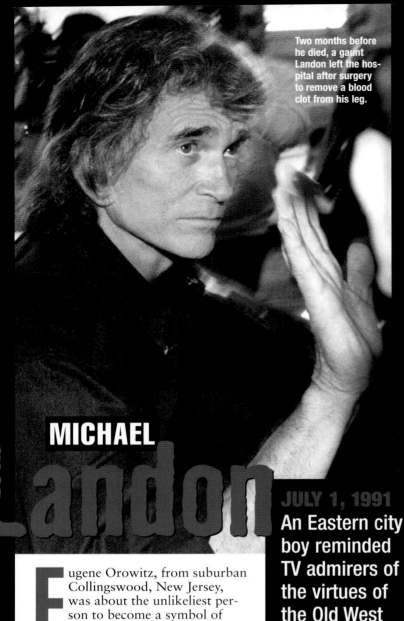

Two months before he died, a gaunt Landon left the hospital after surgery to remove a blood clot from his leg.

MICHAEL
Landon

JULY 1, 1991
An Eastern city boy reminded TV admirers of the virtues of the Old West

Eugene Orowitz, from suburban Collingswood, New Jersey, was about the unlikeliest person to become a symbol of rugged frontier values. His home was unhappy, his anti-Semitic schoolmates tormented him, and the pressure turned him into a chronic bed wetter, who suffered further humiliation when his mother hung the wet sheets out of his bedroom window. College was no more fun. But later, as Michael Landon, his tenacious spirit prevailed. "I've always had to work very hard to be happy," he said, and he worked like a dog. Given the opportunity to act, he played Little Joe, the impulsive Cartwright in *Bonanza,* for 14 years. That gave him the clout to create and honcho *Little House on the Prairie* for nine seasons, then *Highway to Heaven* for five. "His whole thing has always been about control," said his publicist Jay Bernstein. The driven perfectionist had to acknowledge his limitations as he confronted a slow, inevitable death at 54 from liver cancer, caused in part by tobacco and alcohol he had abused over the years to ease his burdens. Surrounded by his nine children from three marriages and his wife, Cindy, Landon was calm, composed, telling jokes and videotaping goodbyes to friends as he faced his ultimate test with a grace that moved the nation.

APRIL 8, 1994 The poet of grunge folds under the weight of sudden fame

Teenage angst has paid off well," Kurt Cobain sang on Nirvana's last studio album. It certainly had. *Nevermind,* the group's breakout album, sold more than 10 million copies. The single "Smells Like Teen Spirit" turned into an anthem. Overnight, Seattle became ground zero for youth culture, and Nirvana was at the top of the grunge heap. Cobain, the group's lead singer and principal writer, was much more than a star—he was a spokesman for his generation.

It was not a role that he had ever sought. A chronic social misfit from a family plagued by suicides, alcoholism and marital problems, he was on Ritalin and sedatives while still a preschooler, and he dropped out of high school just weeks before graduation. Only his musical talent seemed to have saved him from a life of crime. His marriage to the equally hard-living Courtney Love ("We bonded over pharmaceuticals," was her description of their courtship) and the birth of their daughter Frances Bean offered hope of stability. But in the end, Cobain's demons were too strong. On March 29, he abruptly left a drug-recovery center and disappeared. On April 8, his body was found in an apartment over the garage of his house, his head so damaged by the point-blank blast he'd fired that identification had to be made through fingerprints. Eerily like three earlier rock gods—Jimi Hendrix, Janis Joplin and Jim Morrison— Cobain was 27 when he died.

"It's not fun for me anymore. I can't live this life," Cobain wrote in his suicide note. Three months earlier, he had goofed around, poker-faced, for the camera with one of the guns he'd begun to carry around with him.

KURT
Cobain

O.J. SIMPSON

JUNE 17, 1994 As all America watched live, an All-American made a bizarrely decorous end run down a freeway

Al Cowlings, O.J.'s friend since high school, drove the infamous white Bronco and reportedly talked a distraught Simpson out of suicide and into the custody of the LAPD.

Nicole (with O.J. in the '80s) told police she had been beaten during the seven-year union.

It all began in June 1994 as a domestic tragedy among the rich and famous, a double murder confounded by a *Rashomon*-like series of conflicting stories. Then it became a 32-month, national obsession. At the center of the drama stood O.J. Simpson, then 46, football immortal, screen actor and one of the first black athletes to land lucrative endorsements. The victims were his ex-wife, Nicole Brown Simpson, 35, blonde and slim, stabbed so brutally that she was almost decapitated, and Ronald Goldman, 25, a casual acquaintance of hers, the ultimate wrong man in the wrong place at the wrong time.

For Leno and Letterman and pundits across the land, it was a bottomless source of grist. The rest of us pored over the details: the Rockingham estate and the Brentwood mansion, the bloody glove, the noises Kato Kaelin heard outside the guest house. We followed the trial like a soap opera. We had views on everything from prosecutor Marcia Clark's hairstyles to the reliability of DNA evidence.

It was a story without a hero. The prosecution bungled its case. The defense team was a bunch of backbiting prima donnas, who won by playing "the race card." Judge Lance Ito was stagestruck, and the

CLOCKWISE, FROM BOTTOM LEFT: RETNA LTD.; R. HARTOG/THE OUTLOOK/SYGMA; SYGMA; SYGMA POOL

Los Angeles police were incompetent or bigoted or both.

The transformation of Heisman-winning pitchman into pariah has not healed the wounds that Simpson's case opened. Despite the $33.5-million judgment against him in the civil court sequel, the people's verdict on O.J. still runs along a bitter racial divide. Simpson himself is a shadowy figure, popping up on a golf course or out with his children. His epitaph may have been told by an expert in sports memorabilia. Speculating on O.J.'s chances of cashing in on his own holdings, Don Flanagan said, "Anything associated with him is just in bad taste."

Having Simpson try on these Aris gloves, extra-large, in front of the jury was the prosecution's biggest blunder.

After 366 days, Johnnie Cochran Jr. rhymed his summation: "If it doesn't fit, you must acquit." And that's what the jury did.

Jackie
KENNEDY ONASSIS

Ensconced in New York City, Jackie (in the early '90s) relaxed into the roles of working woman, mother and grandmother.

Only 64 when she died, she had outlived her tragedies and made a remarkable life for herself and her children

The First Lady planned every detail of her husband's funeral, with its muffled drums, riderless horse and John Jr.'s heartbreaking salute to the casket.

Taking you anyplace is like going out with a national monument," movie director Mike Nichols once told Jacqueline Bouvier Kennedy Onassis. "Yes," she answered, "but isn't it fun?" No one could resist this patrician Long Island-born beauty with the whispery voice and the self-mocking wit. Her quixotic nature and her extraordinary charisma kept a nation of admirers in rapt awe.

Some of the images in our heads are ineffably sad. The fashion plate with the bouffant hairdo and pillbox hats will always be remembered for the bloodstained pink Chanel suit she refused to take off after her husband, President John F. Kennedy, was murdered in Dallas in 1963. "I want them to see what they've done," she said.

For five years the grieving widow retreated into family life. Then, at 39, she married Aristotle Onassis, the 62-year-old Greek shipping tycoon. Many were dismayed, but as Lee Radziwill explained, "My sister needs a man like Onassis, who can protect her from the curiosity of the world." The need became urgent after Bobby Kennedy's murder in 1968. "If they are killing Kennedys," said Jackie, "my children are the No. 1 targets." They survived, of course. Indeed they flourished, thanks to her masterful mothering. Caroline was 6 and John Jr. only 3 when they lost their father, and they were closely attached to a troubled and troublesome clan of cousins, but nonetheless they grew into responsible adults.

Twice widowed by the time she was 45, Jackie worked diligently at a publishing job, jogged around the Central Park reservoir and periodically sallied forth on behalf of causes like architectural preservation. What she loved most, especially when the lymphoma began to claim her, was quiet time spent with little Rose, Tatiana and Jack (the children of Caroline and husband Edwin Schlossberg) and her devoted last companion, financier Maurice Tempelsman. She was buried at Arlington National Cemetery between her husband Jack and her stillborn daughter. A son (who died in 1963, two days after he was born) lies on Jack's other side.

To raise her family, she moved to Manhattan in 1964. Dignified in the face of paparazzi, she sued Ron Galella (here in 1971).

Jackie delighted in the company of her grown-up children at events like the Profiles in Courage Awards at Boston's JFK Library in 1991.

Selena

MARCH 31, 1995

Her tragic early
death ironically
accelerated
her inevitable
crossover acclaim

Nine months after
Selena's assassination,
fans waited outside a
Houston courthouse
to hear the verdict:
Yolanda Saldivar was
found guilty of first-
degree murder and
sentenced to life.

A sweet, unpretentious 23-year-old with a rambunctious stage act, Selena Quintanilla from Corpus Christie, Texas, was poised on the brink of superstardom. She had emerged as the queen of Tejano music, a giddy mix of Tex-Mex, pop and polka. Hoping to reach beyond her Hispanic audience, Selena had just completed an album with lyrics in English (the language she had grown up with). She was struggling, according to friends, to gain her independence from the controlling father who had pulled her out of school in eighth grade to sing with the family group. Against his wishes, she had married musician Chris Perez, in 1992, and set up boutiques selling the gaudy, revealing clothing she strutted on tour. ("She could do more with a bra and rhinestones than anyone I ever knew," said her friend Rosabel Lopez.)

Selena's then 35-year-old fan club president, Yolanda Saldivar, was in charge of building her business. But on her last, fateful day, Selena went to Saldivar's motel room to accuse her of embezzlement. The gunshot that ended Selena's life got her the hearing that finally won over the Anglo audience, as posthumous sales of her records soared into the millions.

JERRY
Garcia

AUG. 9, 1995

The Deadhead Nation mourned its benevolent Buddha, Captain Trips

J erry Garcia's long, strange trip ended quietly at Serenity Knolls, a drug-treatment center where the 53-year-old guitarist had gone to do battle once again with the heroin addiction that made so much of his adult life a cliff-hanger. Early one morning, his heart simply gave out. The death was, and yet wasn't, a shock. His taste for drugs—pot and acid in the 1960s, giving way to cocaine and heroin by the '80s—was well-documented. So was his reputation for what a Grateful Dead spokesman called a "real bad hot-dog-and-milkshake diet, cigarettes and no exercise for 30 years." In 1986, Garcia had spent a week in a diabetic coma. In 1992, he'd collapsed from exhaustion on tour. But the worst seemed past. His third marriage appeared successful, he had lost weight, taken up scuba diving and gotten closer to his four children. And amazingly, with new generations tuning in, the Dead in 1991 and '93 were the U.S.'s top-grossing live band.

The grieving was global. Deadheads logged on to the Internet by the thousands and held an online wake, posting tribute pages and exchanging condolences. In San Francisco, 25,000 people convened in Golden Gate Park to say farewell in an atmosphere more festive than funereal, a fitting send-off for a man who had led more than a band. He was the patriarch of a cultlike extended family.

Oklahoma City

The worst terrorist attack in U.S. history ripped apart and destroyed the nine-story Alfred P. Murrah Federal Building.

APRIL 19, 1995 A Ryder truck carrying two tons of explosives killed 168 and struck the heart of America

The bomb blast stunned the country. It was the kind of crime that happens abroad, in Ireland or Israel perhaps—but not in Oklahoma. For the first time, terrorists had hit Middle America.

Rumors roiled briefly about suspicious characters seen near the government office building before the explosion, but the manhunt ended at the cell of Timothy McVeigh, a disgruntled Army veteran who had been arrested within hours of the explosion on traffic and weapons charges. McVeigh, then 26, was a far-right extremist with militia ties and a narrow, expressionless face. The criminal was dwarfed by the enormity of his crime.

The whole nation mourned the 168 victims—such as government computer analyst Larry Jones, whose last words that morning to his wife of 19 years had been, "See you later." And Daina Bradley, who lost her mother and her two children along with her leg. And especially the young children whose parents had dropped them off at the daycare center on the building's second floor.

McVeigh was sentenced to death for the bombing, and his conspirator Terry Nichols is serving a life term. But justice cannot repair the lives lost or shattered. Nor can it return our old, innocent belief that such things can't happen here.

The dead included 15 children from the America's Kids daycare center. Six survived, with terrible injuries.

Once upon a time, the most that kids had to worry about at school was a looming test or a deadline for a paper. No more. After the carnage that left 15 dead and 23 wounded at Columbine High in the affluent Denver suburb of Littleton, there can be few youngsters anywhere who feel totally confident that they won't one day encounter a fellow student with a gun in his hand and madness in his eyes. Although the tragedies of West Paducah, Kentucky; Pearl, Mississippi; Jonesboro, Arkansas; and Springfield, Oregon (to name just the most well-known school shootings earlier in the 1990s) were shocking enough, those tolls fell short of the clockwork slaughter among the 1,900 students at Columbine. There, for more than three hours, two misfits spread terror before killing themselves even as hundreds of local, state and federal law-enforcement officers lay siege outside.

The two—Eric Harris, 18, and Dylan Klebold, 17—savored Goth music like Marilyn Manson and violent computer games like Doom as well as Nazi mythology and paraphernalia. They hated the jocks in the rah-rah school who made them feel like outcasts. Klebold, who wore a T-shirt that read SERIAL KILLER the morning of the massacre, is remembered by fellow seniors as a follower in search of a leader. He found one in Harris, who created a Web site on which he had posted bomb-making instructions and virulent warnings to classmates. The parents of Brooks Brown, a senior whom Harris had threatened the previous year, complained to both school and police numerous times, but nothing was ever done.

If Harris and Klebold weren't well-adjusted teens, they still gave few hints of the depths of their lethal alienation. After getting caught stealing in early 1998, they sailed successfully through a juvenile rehabilitation program, and their police records were expunged. Both came from prosperous families, with parents who believed they knew their children well—though Littleton's sheriff wondered aloud on TV how Harris's folks could have ignored the sawed-off shotgun barrel on their son's dresser. There were questions for the police, too, like why it took so long to reach Dave Sanders, 47, the only teacher victim, who heroically herded students to safety before bleeding to death. Thus, Littleton joined the growing list of all-American towns that firmly believed irrational violence could never touch them—until one day, it did.

APRIL 20, 1999 **The killers' long, dark coats concealed an arsenal—and a horrifying rage**

Columbine

Like refugees just escaped from a war zone, Columbine students (left) awaited word on friends still trapped inside. Patrick Ireland (above), 17, was bleeding badly from head wounds but had the presence of mind to make this daring escape. A policeman (below) helped a wounded student at the triage station outside the school.

◄ **Dubbed the Trenchcoat Mafia** for their rebel garb, Klebold (far left, in '98) drove a BMW. Harris (left, in '99) was taking the antidepressant Luvox to treat an obsessive compulsive disorder. In the course of their onslaught, the pair fired some 900 rounds, planted homemade bombs throughout the school and then booby-trapped their own bodies.

➤ **Isaiah Shoels** (right in '93), 18, overcame childhood heart problems to become a promising athlete. Taunted by the assailants previously, he was one of 16 blacks in the school and the only one to die in the tragedy. During the attack, one of the killers asked Cassie Bernall (far right, in '98), 17, "Do you believe in God?" She said she did, and he shot her in the head.

THE AIDS
CRISIS

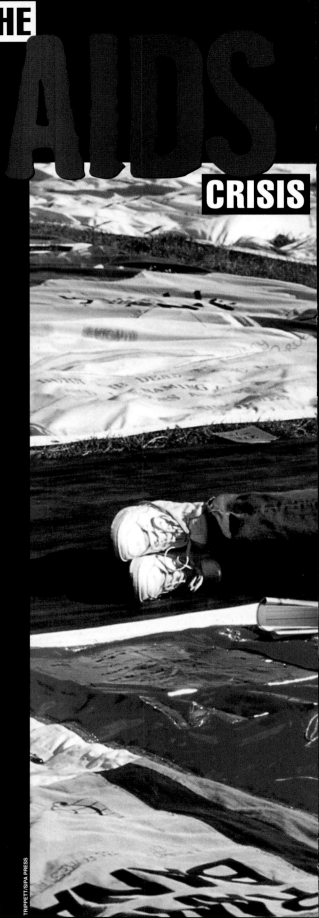

I t first gained our attention on the West Coast in 1980, when once-healthy gay men began succumbing to rare forms of cancer and pneumonia. In 1983, the Centers for Disease Control discovered that the HIV virus was causing these fatalities by destroying the body's immune system. By the following year, with 10 new cases logged each week in the U.S., it was given the name AIDS (Acquired Immuno-deficiency Syndrome). By 1996, the yearly rate of new AIDS cases ranged between 40,000 and 80,000, and an estimated 343,000 Americans had already died. As the AIDS epidemic destroyed lives, it also raised myriad public health and moral questions. In the conservative '80s, the country had to confront such unsettling issues as safe sex, gay sex—and the distribution of condoms to teens and clean needles to drug addicts.

ONGOING
Twenty years into a tragic epidemic, the world reflects —and rethinks its mores and sex practices

Starting as a disease of monkeys in Zaire, AIDS had spread by the 1950s to humans, and by the '70s from Africa to the gay populations of California and New York, where it thrived, undetected, for years. It defied cure. Famous victims, as well as people in our own neighborhoods and families, brought the affliction to the forefront. The virus was in the nation's blood supply. Mothers unwittingly passed it to their babies, husbands to their wives, health care workers to patients. The shocks kept coming. People kept dying.

In recent years there has been some progress, including the development of potent drug cocktails that keep people alive. The U.S. blood supply is now clean, but the crisis continues. Education cuts the U.S. infection rate; then, with overconfidence, it climbs again. In parts of Africa, as much as 25 percent of the population is HIV-positive. Domestically, AIDS deaths are rising among those poor and minorities who don't have access to information or to the costly medication that can keep the disease at bay. And so far, for all the lab research, there is no sign of a vaccine.

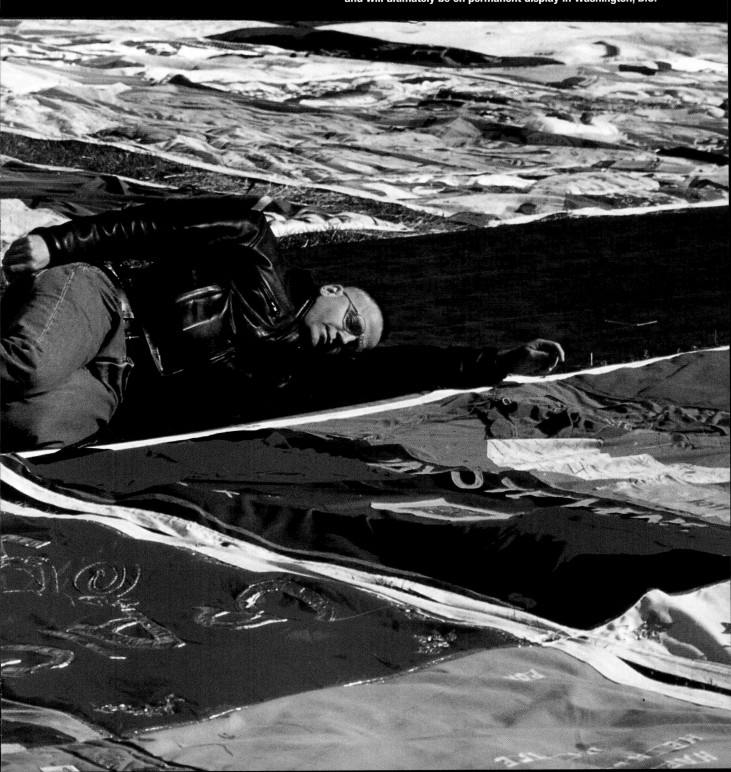

THE AIDS QUILT A mourner paid his respects in 1996 at the patchwork started 11 years before in San Francisco. It contains more than 41,000 panels, with a few hundred more added monthly, each representing an AIDS death. At latest count, it weighed 52 tons and will ultimately be on permanent display in Washington, D.C.

ROCK HUDSON In July 1985, three months before he died, the ailing, 59-year-old actor posed with his former costar Doris Day to publicize her new TV show. Days later, after experimental treatment failed, he announced that he had AIDS, ending his secret life and changing his image forever. The day Hudson died, Congress voted to allocate $189.7 million for AIDS research.

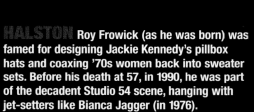

HALSTON Roy Frowick (as he was born) was famed for designing Jackie Kennedy's pillbox hats and coaxing '70s women back into sweater sets. Before his death at 57, in 1990, he was part of the decadent Studio 54 scene, hanging with jet-setters like Bianca Jagger (in 1976).

RYAN WHITE He lived five-and-a-half years after he was diagnosed at 12. A hemophiliac who had contracted AIDS from a transfusion, this skinny boy with the sturdy spirit fought the Kokomo, Indiana, school board for keeping him out of class, fought public prejudice with his candor and humor, fought his disease with the support of luminary friends such as Elton John and Michael Jackson and with the love of his mother, Jeanne. Ryan (in 1985) just wanted to be normal again. "It's creepy," he wrote, "to be famous because you're sick."

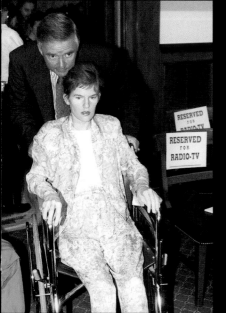

KIMBERLY BERGALIS "I just went to the dentist," she insisted. During a tooth extraction, that dentist, David Acer, infected Bergalis with the AIDS virus—and also four more of his patients. In 1991 she died, at 23, after testifying (here, with her lawyer) in Washington, D.C., on behalf of mandatory testing of health care workers.

ARTHUR ASHE In 1992 he calmly told the world he was HIV-positive as his wife, photographer Jeanne Moutoussamy-Ashe, stood by. He had become infected after open-heart surgery in 1983. The first black man to win Wimbledon and the U.S. Open, Ashe was a powerful spokesman for human rights. He campaigned for AIDS awareness until his death, at 49, in 1993. As a last, loving act, he left letters for daughter Camera, then 6.

ELIZABETH GLASER A schoolteacher who married a celebrity, Paul Michael Glaser of *Starsky and Hutch*, she became HIV-positive from transfusions after the birth of her daughter Ariel, in 1981, and passed the virus on to Ariel and son Jake through her breast milk. After Ariel died of AIDS, at 7, Glaser became an indomitable activist. She spoke out at the Democratic Convention in 1992 and cofounded the Pediatric Aids Foundation, hoping that somehow she could save her son. Glaser died, at 47, in 1994. Jake, 15, is presently doing well on powerful HIV inhibitors.

INDEX